FALCONRIDGE SCHOOL

FALCONRIDGE SCHOOL

FALCONRIDGE SCHOOL

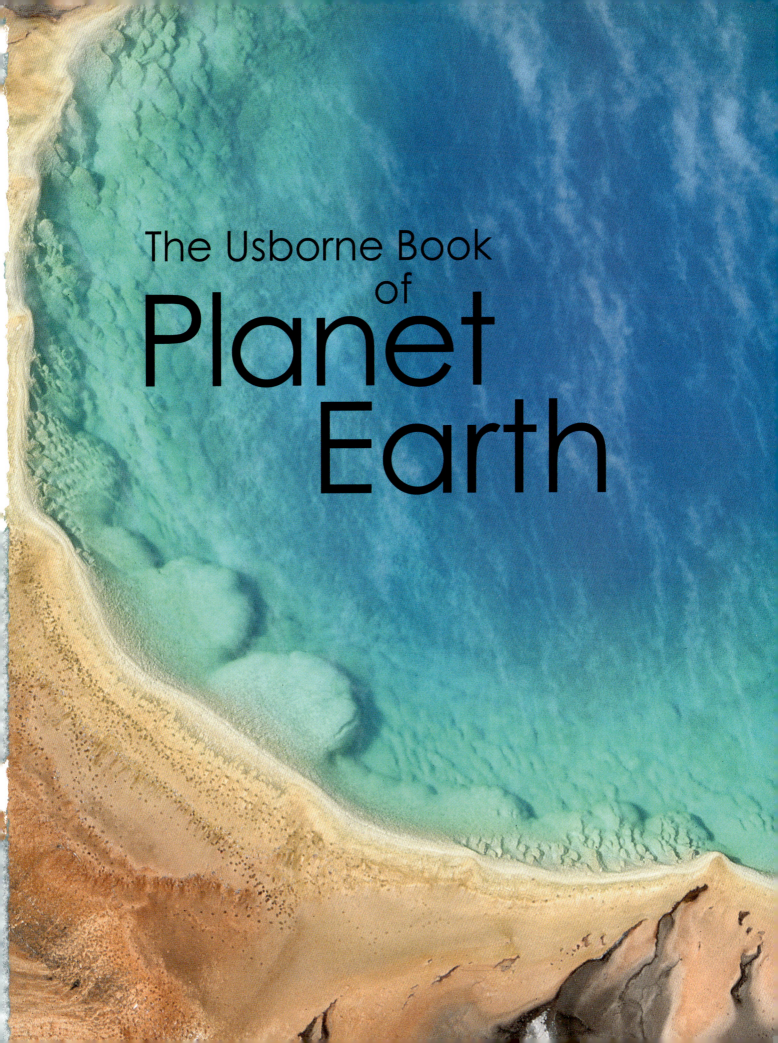

The Usborne Book of Planet Earth

The Usborne Book of Planet Earth

Anna Claybourne, Gillian Doherty and Rebecca Treays

Designed by Laura Fearn and Melissa Alaverdy

Consultant: Dr. William Chambers

Cover design: Zoe Wray and Louise Bartlett

Digital images: John Russell and Nicola Butler

Picture research: Ruth King

Page 1: aerial view of the Grand Prismatic Spring, Yellowstone National Park, USA
Pages 2–3: the Chicago skyline, USA
This page: computer-enhanced image of an iceberg

CONTENTS

Planet Earth

- 8 The Earth in Space
- 10 Looking at the Earth
- 12 The Seasons
- 14 Day and Night
- 16 Inside the Earth
- 18 The Earth's Crust
- 20 Rocks, Minerals and Fossils
- 22 The Earth's Resources
- 24 Energy from the Earth

Earthquakes and Volcanoes

- 28 The Exploding Earth
- 30 Volcanic Variations
- 32 Natural Hot Water
- 34 Volcanic Islands
- 36 Living with Volcanoes
- 38 Earthquake Effects
- 40 How Earthquakes Happen
- 42 Earthquake Safety
- 44 Giant Waves

Climate

- 48 The Earth's Atmosphere
- 50 Air and Ocean Currents
- 52 Natural Cycles
- 54 Global Warming
- 56 World Climates
- 58 Rainforests
- 60 Tropical Grasslands
- 62 Monsoons
- 64 Tropical Deserts
- 66 Mediterranean Climates
- 68 Temperate Climates
- 70 Polar Regions
- 72 Mountains
- 74 Changing Climates

Weather

- 78 What is Weather?
- 80 Water and Clouds
- 82 Thunderstorms
- 84 Windstorms
- 86 Floods and Droughts
- 88 Freezing and Frying
- 90 Strange Weather
- 92 Weather Forecasting

Plants and Animals

- 96 Plant Life on Earth
- 98 Animal Life on Earth
- 100 Ecosystems
- 102 People and Ecosystems
- 104 Population
- 106 Farming
- 108 Farming Methods

Shaping the Land

- 112 Soil
- 114 Looking after Soil
- 116 Weathering
- 118 Erosion

Rivers and Oceans

- 122 Rivers
- 124 River Erosion
- 126 Using Rivers
- 128 Water in the Ground
- 130 Rivers of Ice
- 132 The Edge of the Sea
- 134 Seas and Oceans
- 136 Using Seas and Oceans

Useful Information

- 140 Glossary
- 146 Maps and Lines
- 148 The Earth's Cycles
- 150 Geographers and Scientists
- 152 World Records
- 154 Measurements
- 155 Usborne Quicklinks
- 156 Index

Some words in this book have an asterisk* after them. This means that you can find out more about them on the page listed in the footnote.

Internet links

This book contains descriptions of websites where you can find out more about Planet Earth. To visit the sites, go to the Usborne Quicklinks website at www.usborne.com/quicklinks and enter the keywords "planet earth". Pictures marked in this book with a ★ symbol can be downloaded at Usborne Quicklinks for your own personal use. Please read our internet safety guidelines at the Usborne Quicklinks website. For more information about Usborne Quicklinks and the internet, see page 155.

The Earth and its moon

PLANET EARTH

THE EARTH IN SPACE

The Earth may seem enormous, but it's actually just a tiny speck in a universe made up of trillions of stars and planets. Its position in relation to the Sun is very important. The Sun provides the heat and light that we need to survive.

The Sun
Mercury
Venus
Earth
Mars
Jupiter
Saturn
Neptune
Uranus

This picture shows the eight planets in our solar system in the correct order, although they are not to scale.

The universe is everything; not just the trillions of stars and planets, but the vast spaces in between.

Our solar system

Stars are huge balls of hot gas that give off heat and light. Most look tiny, but that's just because they are so far away. The nearest star to Earth is the Sun.

A planet is an object that travels around, or orbits, a star. As each planet moves, it also spins around on its own axis (an imaginary line running through the planet). The Earth is one of eight planets and other smaller objects orbiting the Sun. Together they make up our solar system.

The Earth spins around on its axis as it orbits the Sun.

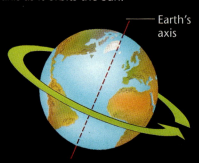

Earth's axis

Internet links

For links to websites about space with amazing pictures of the Sun, go to
www.usborne.com/quicklinks

The Moon

Most of the planets in our solar system have moons. A moon orbits a planet in the same way that a planet orbits a star. Earth has just one moon, but some planets, such as Saturn, have many. It takes almost 28 days for the Moon to orbit the Earth.

As the Moon orbits the Earth, it rotates. It takes exactly the same amount of time to spin around once as it does to travel around the Earth. This means that when we look at the Moon from the Earth, we always see the same side of it.

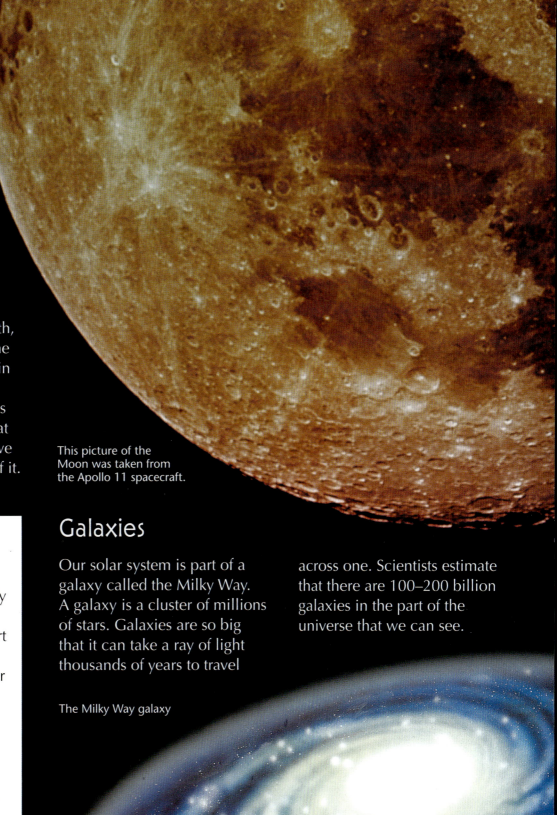

This picture of the Moon was taken from the Apollo 11 spacecraft.

Living Earth

Earth is the third planet from the Sun. It is the only known planet with the right conditions to support living things, although scientists are searching for life on other planets.

The Earth's distance from the Sun means that it receives just the right amount of heat and light. Its combination of gases enables plants, animals and people to breathe, and it is warm enough for water to exist as a liquid. All of these things are essential for life on Earth.

Galaxies

Our solar system is part of a galaxy called the Milky Way. A galaxy is a cluster of millions of stars. Galaxies are so big that it can take a ray of light thousands of years to travel across one. Scientists estimate that there are 100–200 billion galaxies in the part of the universe that we can see.

The Milky Way galaxy

LOOKING AT THE EARTH

We now have a more accurate picture of the world than ever before. Modern technology has meant that scientists can monitor vast areas of the Earth from space. Even inaccessible places, such as deserts, ocean floors and mountain ranges, have been mapped in detail.

Dividing lines

On maps, imaginary lines are used to divide up the Earth. These help us to measure distances and find where places are. The lines that run horizontally are called lines of latitude and the lines that run vertically are known as lines of longitude. The distance between the lines is measured in degrees (°).

Some of the lines used to divide up the Earth have special names. The most important ones are shown on this globe.

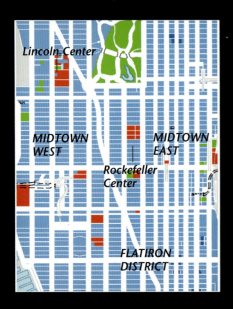

A map showing the layout of streets in Manhattan, New York, USA.

Flattening the Earth's surface

Because the Earth is roughly spherical, the best way to represent it accurately is as a globe. In order to produce flat maps of the Earth's surface, cartographers (map-makers) have to stretch some areas and squash others. Different kinds of maps give the countries slightly different shapes and sizes. These different views of the Earth's surface are called projections*.

The most accurate flat map of the world looks like pieces of orange peel.

Maps of the Earth

A map is a diagram which gives information about a particular area. Maps can show anything from road layouts to the shape of the land. Some focus on small areas, but others show the whole of the Earth's surface. The size of a map in relation to the area it represents is called its scale. If a map's scale is 1:100, it shows an area 100 times its size.

*Projections, 147

Artificial satellites are man-made devices which orbit the Earth, moons, or other planets. They observe the Earth using a technique called remote sensing. This means that instruments on the satellite monitor the Earth without touching it. Some satellites orbit the Earth at a height of between 5km (3 miles) and 1500km (930 miles), providing views of different parts of the Earth. Others stay above the same place all the time, moving at the same speed as the Earth to give a constant view of a particular area. These are called geostationary satellites. They travel at a height of around 36,000km (22,370 miles).

Sensing

Satellites use a range of remote sensing techniques. One useful type is radar. It can provide images of the Earth even when it is dark or cloudy. Radar works by reflecting radio waves off a target object. The time it takes for a wave to bounce back indicates how far away the object is.

Cameras are used to photograph the Earth's surface. The images are converted into electrical pulses and beamed to Earth. Some cameras use a form of radiation known as infrared. Different types of surfaces reflect infrared light differently, so it's possible to obtain images of the Earth which show the varieties of land surfaces. This can be useful for monitoring vegetation.

Prime Meridian line

This Sentinel satellite is used to collect information to help scientists study climate change.

Internet links

For links to websites about satellites go to **www.usborne.com/quicklinks**

Satellite uses

Information provided by satellites enables experts to produce accurate maps, predict hazards such as volcanic eruptions or earthquakes, and record changes in land use around the world. Sensors can also reveal day-to-day changes, such as whether soil is wet or dry, and for monitoring weather.

This satellite image of the Earth shows its different types of land surfaces.

THE SEASONS

The Earth takes just over a year to orbit the Sun. As it makes its journey, different parts of the world receive different amounts of heat and light. This causes the seasons (spring, summer, autumn and winter).

Tilting Earth

The Earth is tilted at an angle as it travels around the Sun. This means that one half, or hemisphere, is usually closer to the Sun than the other. The hemisphere that is closer receives more heat and light energy than the one that is tilted away. So in this half it is summer, while in the other it is winter.

As the Earth orbits the Sun, the half that was closer to the Sun gradually moves farther away, so that eventually it becomes winter in this hemisphere and summer in the other. In June the Sun's rays are most concentrated at the Tropic of Cancer and in December they are most concentrated at the Tropic of Capricorn.

In June, it is summer in the Arctic. The warmer weather only lasts for six to eight weeks.

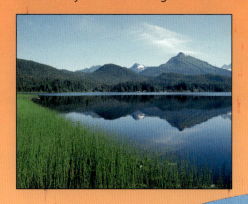

In autumn in Maine, northeast USA, the leaves on the trees turn red and golden.

The diagram below shows how the seasons change as the Earth orbits the Sun.

March: Neither hemisphere is tilted toward the Sun.

June: When the northern hemisphere is tilted toward the Sun, it is summer there. In the southern hemisphere, it is winter.

September: As in March, neither hemisphere is tilted toward the Sun.

December: When the northern hemisphere is tilted away from the Sun, it is winter there. In the southern hemisphere, it is summer.

The heat and light that the Sun gives out are essential for life on Earth.

Leap years

The time it takes for the Earth to orbit the Sun is called a solar year. A solar year is 365.26 days, but as it is more convenient to measure our calendar year in whole days, we round the number down to 365. In order to make up the difference, every four years we have to add an extra day to our calendar year, making it 366 days. These years are called leap years*. The additional day is February 29th. However, this does not make up the difference exactly, so very occasionally the extra day is not added.

Equatorial seasons

The Earth is hottest where the Sun's rays hit its surface full on. But because the Earth's surface is curved, in most places rays hit the ground at an angle. This causes them to spread out over a larger area, which makes their effect less intense.

Temperatures are also affected by the distance the Sun's rays have to travel through the Earth's atmosphere. Over greater distances, the Sun's rays lose more heat energy to the atmosphere, which makes temperatures cooler.

This picture shows how the Sun's rays spread out as they reach the Earth's surface.

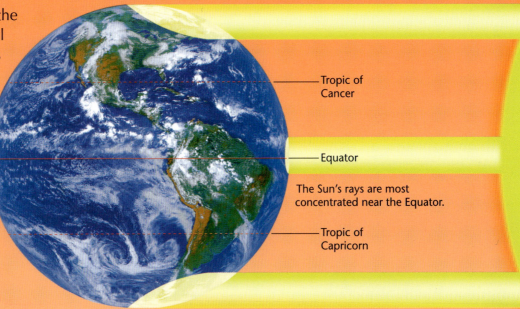

- Tropic of Cancer
- Equator

The Sun's rays are most concentrated near the Equator.

- Tropic of Capricorn

The Sun's rays spread out at the poles and have farther to travel through the Earth's atmosphere.

Internet links

For links to websites with video clips, photographs and fascinating facts about how the seasons change as the Earth travels around the Sun, go to www.usborne.com/quicklinks

At the poles, the midday Sun is low on the horizon even in summer, making it cool.

At the Equator, the midday Sun is high in the sky all year round, so it is very hot.

*Leap years, 148

DAY AND NIGHT

When it's daytime in Australia, it's night-time in South America. This is because the Earth spins around on its axis as it orbits the Sun, so the part of the Earth that faces the Sun is constantly changing.

Rotating Earth

It takes 24 hours, or one day, for the Earth to spin around once on its axis. As it rotates, different parts of the world turn to face the Sun. The part of the Earth that is turned toward the Sun is in the light (daytime), but as it turns away from the Sun it becomes dark (night-time).

This diagram follows the change from day to night in one place (marked by the flag) as the Earth spins.

Path of orbit around the Sun

Sunrise and sunset

In the morning, you see the Sun "rise" in the sky. This is only an illusion. What is actually happening is that as your part of the Earth is turning to face the Sun, the movement of the Earth makes it seem as though the Sun is rising. When your part of the Earth turns away from the Sun at night, it looks as if the Sun is sinking in the sky until eventually it disappears over the horizon. This is called a sunset.

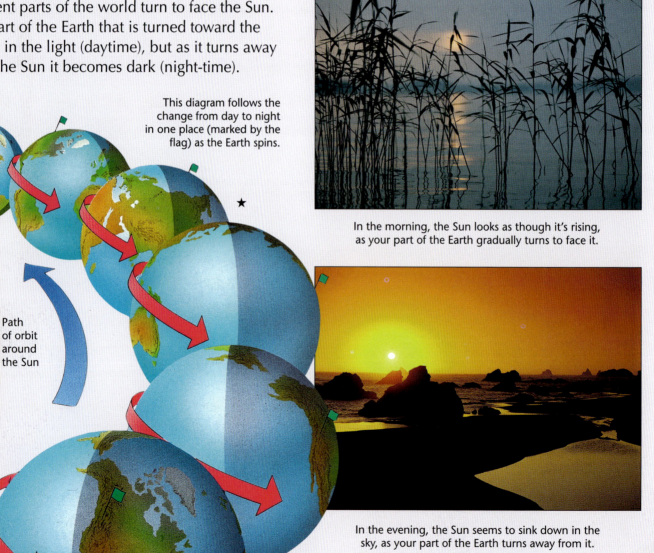

In the morning, the Sun looks as though it's rising, as your part of the Earth gradually turns to face it.

In the evening, the Sun seems to sink down in the sky, as your part of the Earth turns away from it.

Daylight hours

Everywhere in the world, apart from places that are on the Equator, days are longer in the summer than in the winter. This is because the hemisphere where it is summer receives more sunlight than the hemisphere where it is winter.

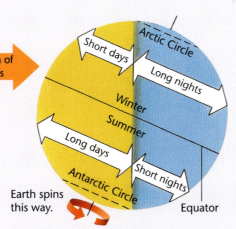

This diagram shows how the length of day and night varies depending on the time of year and where you are on the Earth.

Midnight Sun

In summer, when the northern hemisphere tilts toward the Sun, the regions north of the Arctic Circle don't turn away from the Sun, even at night. For this reason it is known as the Land of the Midnight Sun.

This shows the Sun in the Arctic Circle in the middle of the night.

Internet links

For links to websites where you can see regions on Earth where it is day and night right now, watch videos about the Midnight Sun and see images of the phases of the Moon, go to www.usborne.com/quicklinks

Moon shapes

The Moon doesn't give out any light of its own. It looks bright to us because we see the Sun's rays reflected off its surface.

As the Moon orbits the Sun and we see different amounts of its sunlit side, its shape seems to change as shown in these diagrams.

The pictures below show what the Moon looks like from the northern hemisphere when it is in each of the positions numbered above. When the Moon is visible from the southern hemisphere, the sequence is reversed, so that a southern waxing Moon looks like a northern waning Moon. On the Equator, a crescent Moon may appear to lie on its back.

- 1. New Moon
- 2. Waxing crescent
- 3. First quarter
- 4. Waxing gibbous
- 5. Full Moon
- 6. Waning gibbous
- 7. Last quarter
- 8. Waning crescent

INSIDE THE EARTH

The Earth is mainly solid. It has a rocky surface, but inside it has different layers, some of which are partly molten (melted). If you sliced through the Earth, you would see four main layers: the crust, the mantle, the outer core and the inner core.

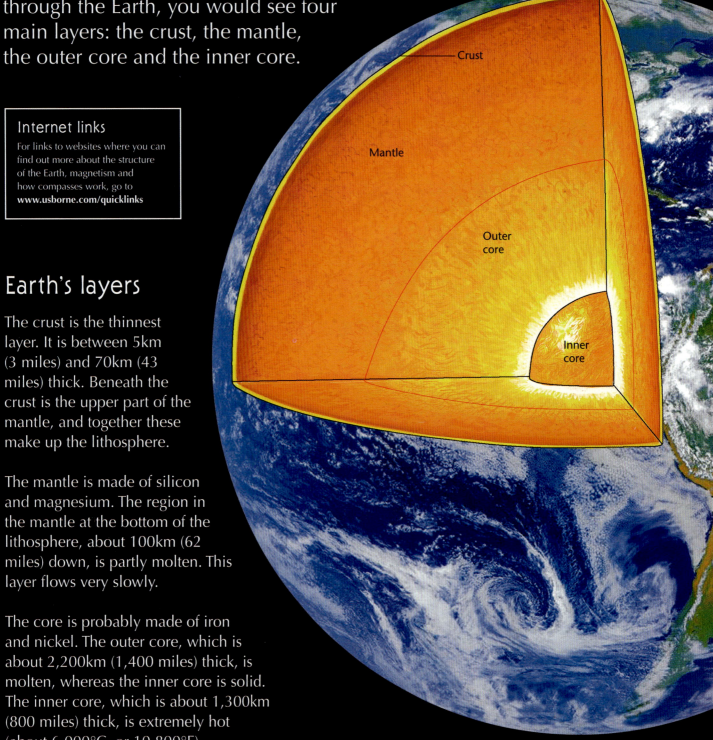

This diagram shows the Earth's structure, though the layers are not drawn to scale.

Internet links

For links to websites where you can find out more about the structure of the Earth, magnetism and how compasses work, go to www.usborne.com/quicklinks

Earth's layers

The crust is the thinnest layer. It is between 5km (3 miles) and 70km (43 miles) thick. Beneath the crust is the upper part of the mantle, and together these make up the lithosphere.

The mantle is made of silicon and magnesium. The region in the mantle at the bottom of the lithosphere, about 100km (62 miles) down, is partly molten. This layer flows very slowly.

The core is probably made of iron and nickel. The outer core, which is about 2,200km (1,400 miles) thick, is molten, whereas the inner core is solid. The inner core, which is about 1,300km (800 miles) thick, is extremely hot (about 6,000°C, or 10,800°F).

The Earth's crust

There are two different types of crust. Thick continental crust forms land, and much thinner oceanic crust makes up the ocean floors. Continental crust is made of granite and similar light rocks. Oceanic crust is made of a heavier rock called basalt.

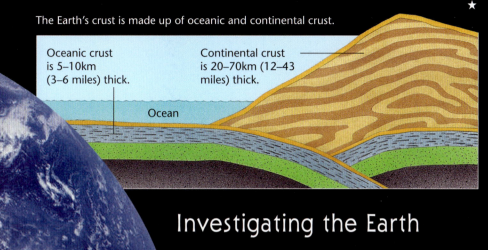

The Earth's crust is made up of oceanic and continental crust.

Oceanic crust is 5–10km (3–6 miles) thick.

Continental crust is 20–70km (12–43 miles) thick.

Ocean

Investigating the Earth

It's difficult to find out about the inside of the Earth. Geologists, who study rocks, find out about areas near the surface by drilling holes into the crust and collecting rock samples. But they can only drill a short distance below the surface.

Volcanic eruptions provide some information about material deep inside the Earth. But the main way that geologists find out about the Earth's structure is by studying earthquakes. During an earthquake, vibrations called seismic waves travel through the Earth. As they pass through different materials, they change speed and direction. By studying records of earthquakes, called seismograms, geologists try to determine what rocks are found at different depths.

Earthquake

Paths of waves

This diagram shows how seismic waves change direction as they pass through the Earth.

Magnetic Earth

The Earth is magnetic, as if it had a huge magnetic bar inside. This may be caused by molten iron circulating in its core. The ends of this "magnet" are called the magnetic poles. These are not in exactly the same place as the geographic North and South Poles.

This diagram shows the Earth's magnetic field: the field of force surrounding it. The lines show the direction of the magnetic field.

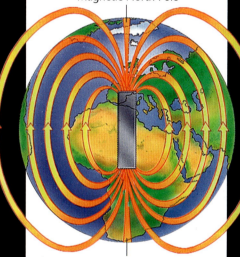

Magnetic North Pole

Magnetic South Pole

You can see the Earth's magnetism at work when you use a compass. The compass needle, which is magnetic, always points north. This is because it is pulled, or attracted, by the magnetic North Pole.

A compass's magnetic needle always points north.

THE EARTH'S CRUST

The solid surface of the Earth is broken up into large pieces called lithospheric plates, which are made up of the Earth's crust and upper mantle. Many of the Earth's most spectacular features have been formed by the movement of these plates.

A moving surface

There are seven large plates and several smaller plates. The edges of the plates are called plate boundaries. The plates move on the partly molten layer of the mantle at a rate of about 5cm (2in) a year. As all the plates fit together, movement of one plate affects the others. The study of these plates and the way they move around is called plate tectonics.

Internet links
To watch video clips about the Earth's tectonic plates and see how they may have shifted over time to create the continents, go to www.usborne.com/quicklinks

Ocean features

As plates on the ocean floor move apart, molten rock, or magma, from the mantle rises and fills the gap. Boundaries where this happens are called constructive boundaries. As the magma reaches the surface, it hardens to make new oceanic crust. The new crust sometimes forms islands or underwater mountain ranges, called ridges.

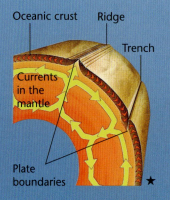

When plates push together, underwater trenches form as one plate is forced below another. These boundaries are called destructive boundaries. The deepest trench, the Mariana Trench in the Pacific Ocean, is deeper than Mount Everest is tall.

This diagram shows how ridges and trenches form.

Shifting continents

As plates shift, the position of the oceans and continents on the Earth's surface changes. The maps on the right show how geologists think the continents may have shifted.

Geologists think that there was once a single supercontinent, which we call "Pangaea".

As new rock formed at plate boundaries, the floor of the Atlantic Ocean probably widened.

Today, South America and Africa are drifting apart at a rate of 3.5cm (1.5in) each year.

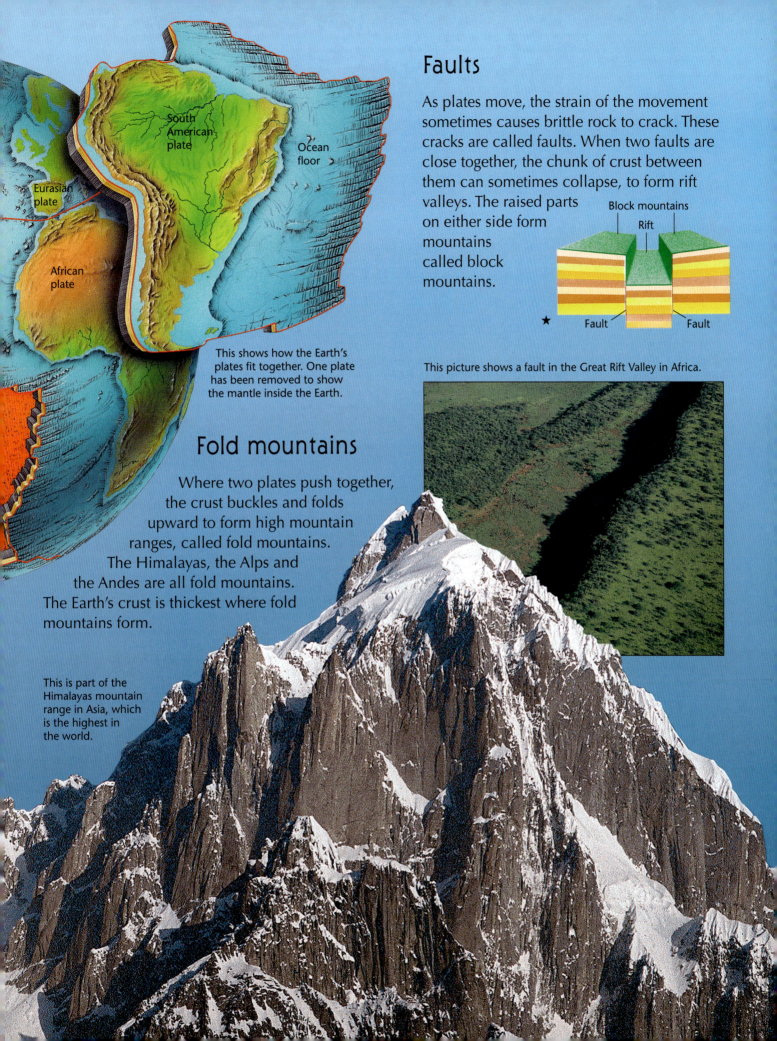

This shows how the Earth's plates fit together. One plate has been removed to show the mantle inside the Earth.

Faults

As plates move, the strain of the movement sometimes causes brittle rock to crack. These cracks are called faults. When two faults are close together, the chunk of crust between them can sometimes collapse, to form rift valleys. The raised parts on either side form mountains called block mountains.

This picture shows a fault in the Great Rift Valley in Africa.

Fold mountains

Where two plates push together, the crust buckles and folds upward to form high mountain ranges, called fold mountains. The Himalayas, the Alps and the Andes are all fold mountains. The Earth's crust is thickest where fold mountains form.

This is part of the Himalayas mountain range in Asia, which is the highest in the world.

ROCKS, MINERALS AND FOSSILS

The Earth's crust is made up of rock. There are three kinds of rocks: igneous, sedimentary and metamorphic. Over many years, rocks are sometimes transformed from one kind to another.

Igneous rock

Igneous rock gets its name from the Latin word for "fire", because it is formed from magma from inside the Earth. When the magma cools, it forms solid igneous rock. The way that the magma cools determines the hardness and appearance of the igneous rock that is formed.

Sedimentary rock

Sedimentary rock is made from tiny pieces of rocks and the decayed remains of plants and animals. These fragments, called sediment, are usually blown by winds, or carried by rivers, glaciers or landslides, to the sea, where they sink. The water and upper layers of sediment press down on the lower layers until, eventually, they form solid rock.

Chalk is a sedimentary rock made from tiny sea creatures.

Tuff is an igneous rock made from pieces of volcanic rock and crystals compressed together.

Obsidian is a shiny igneous rock formed when magma cools quickly.

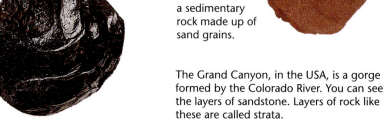

Sandstone is a sedimentary rock made up of sand grains.

The Grand Canyon, in the USA, is a gorge formed by the Colorado River. You can see the layers of sandstone. Layers of rock like these are called strata.

Metamorphic rock

Metamorphic rock is rock that has been changed – for example, by heat from magma, or pressure caused by plate movements or very deep burial. It can be formed from igneous, sedimentary or other metamorphic rocks.

Marble is a metamorphic rock formed from limestone.

Mica schist is a metamorphic rock that tends to split into layers.

Minerals

Rocks are made from substances called minerals, which in turn are made up of simple chemical substances called elements. Some minerals are cut and polished to be used as gemstones.

These pictures show minerals in rocks and as gemstones.

Opal can be milky white, green, red, blue, black or brown.

Turquoise runs through rock in the form of veins.

Carnelian is a dark red stone.

Internet links

For links to websites with video clips about different kinds of rocks and how fossils form, go to www.usborne.com/quicklinks

Fossils

The shapes or remains of plants and animals that died long ago are sometimes preserved in rocks. They are called fossils. Fossils are formed when a dead plant or animal is buried by sediment which then turns to sedimentary rock. Usually the remains decay, although hard parts such as teeth, shells and bones can sometimes survive. The space left by the plant or animal fills up with sediment or minerals which preserve its shape.

The fossil of an ammonite (an extinct sea creature)

THE EARTH'S RESOURCES

The Earth provides all sorts of useful rocks, minerals and other materials. We quarry stone and sand for building and glassmaking, extract over 60 types of metals, and mine hundreds of useful chemicals and compounds such as salt, talc and silicon.

Metals and minerals

Metals are among the most important materials we get from the Earth. They are strong, yet they can be beaten out into flat sheets or drawn out to make wire. They also conduct electricity and heat well. Some metals even have medical uses.

Most metals are found in ores, types of rocks that contain a metal in the form of a chemical compound. Metals are extracted from ores by mixing them with other chemicals to cause a reaction or by heating them strongly.

As well as metals and stone, the Earth also provides many other chemicals and elements. Their uses often depend on how hard they are.

People have used precious metals for centuries as settings for precious stones.

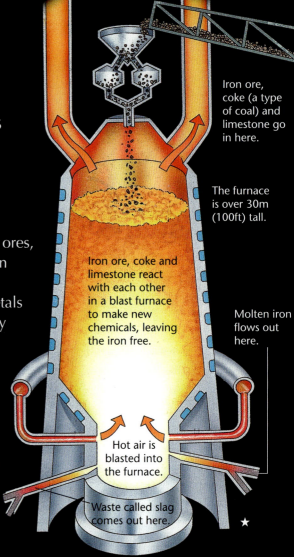

Iron is extracted from its ore in a blast furnace.

Iron ore, coke (a type of coal) and limestone go in here.

The furnace is over 30m (100ft) tall.

Iron ore, coke and limestone react with each other in a blast furnace to make new chemicals, leaving the iron free.

Molten iron flows out here.

Hot air is blasted into the furnace.

Waste called slag comes out here.

Internet links

To zoom into a silicon chip, watch an animation of a blast furnace and find activities about metals and minerals, including a recipe for growing your own crystals, go to **www.usborne.com/quicklinks**

The Mohs scale

The hardness or softness of minerals is measured on a scale of 1 to 10, called the Mohs scale. Soft minerals, such as talc, crumble easily into powder. At the other end of the scale are the hardest minerals, such as diamonds, which are used in cutting tools.

Talc 1
Gypsum 2
Calcite 3
Fluorite 4

Each number on the Mohs scale is accompanied by an example mineral.

Apatite 5
Orthoclase 6
Quartz 7
Topaz 8
Corundum 9
Diamond 10

Silicon chips

Silicon comes from a mineral called quartz. It has become very important in modern society, because it is used to make the electronic chips that run computers, digital watches, mobile phones and millions of other everyday appliances.

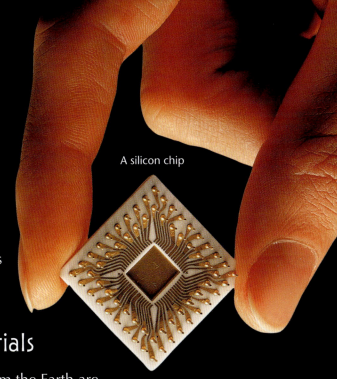

A silicon chip

Building materials

Rocks and minerals from the Earth are used to make bricks, cement, glass and other building materials. Stone for building is usually extracted from the ground in quarries. It's often so hard and heavy that explosives have to be used to blast it apart.

Sand is made of rocks, minerals and sometimes seashells, ground down to fragments by the action of water (which is why it is usually found near the sea). Concrete and glass are both made using sand.

The Taj Mahal is a huge Indian tomb. Its exterior is white marble.

ENERGY FROM THE EARTH

The Earth's rocks, minerals and fossils contain energy which we can extract and use. Oil, gas and coal, which can be converted into heat and electricity, all come from the Earth. So do other forms of energy, such as nuclear energy.

This huge structure is the top part of an oil platform, which sticks out above the sea's surface. It contains equipment for processing the oil, and living quarters for the workers.

Fossil fuels

Coal, oil and natural gas are fossil fuels. They are called this because, like fossils*, they form in the ground over a very long period of time from the bodies of dead plants and animals.

Coal is formed from trees and other plants. Layers of sand and clay gradually settled on top of them, and compressed them slowly into thick, underground layers, or seams, of coal.

Oil is formed from the bodies of tiny sea creatures. It is usually found in rocks under the seabed but may be found under land. Under certain conditions, natural gas is formed from dead plants and animals. Gas and oil are often found close together.

Extracting fuels

The coal we use comes from underground mines or opencast mines, which are huge, open holes dug in the ground. To extract oil and gas, a drill, supported by a structure called a rig, bores a hole into the ground or seabed. Sometimes the fuel flows out naturally, but usually water is pumped into the hole to force the oil or gas out.

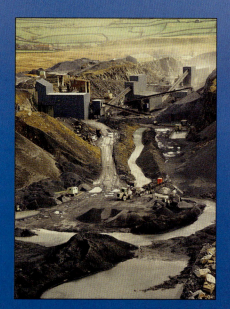

Coal being extracted from a mine at the surface of the ground, called an open cast mine.

*Fossils, 21.

Using fossil fuels

When a fossil fuel is burned, it releases energy, which is used to heat buildings and to run vehicle engines. In power stations, heat from fossil fuels is converted into electricity.

The world depends on fossil fuels. They provide more than three-quarters of the energy we use. But we use them up more quickly than they can form, so they are running out. In less than two hundred years, humans will need to get most of their energy in other ways.

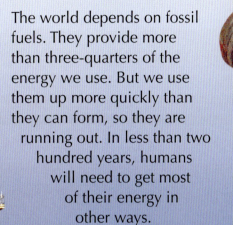

As well as providing energy, oil is used to make plastic, which is made into thousands of things, from bottles to polyester clothing.

Radiation

Some minerals found in the ground are radioactive. This means their atoms (the tiny particles they are made of) are unstable.

Instead of staying as they are, unstable minerals break up and send out particles or rays, known as radiation. As they break up, a type of energy called nuclear energy is released. Uranium, a metal, is the main radioactive mineral used to produce nuclear energy.

Internet links

For links to websites about fossil fuels, how they're extracted and what we use them for, go to
www.usborne.com/quicklinks

This diagram shows how atoms of uranium produce nuclear energy.

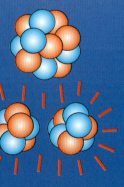

A tiny particle called a neutron is fired at the uranium nucleus.

This is the nucleus, or middle, of a uranium atom.

The nucleus splits, giving off energy.

More neutrons fly off the nucleus and split other uranium atoms.

Lava flowing from the Kilauea volcano, Hawaii

EARTHQUAKES AND VOLCANOES

THE EXPLODING EARTH

An erupting volcano is one of the most dramatic sights in the natural world. Bubbling hot lava spews out of a hole in the Earth's crust and engulfs the land. Ash, dust and poisonous gases pour into the air and chunks of rock are hurled high into the sky.

Volcanoes

Volcanoes erupt when red-hot molten rock, called magma, from the Earth's mantle rises toward the surface. Eventually it builds up enough pressure to burst through the Earth's crust. Once magma has reached the surface of the Earth it is called lava.

A cross-section through a cone volcano

Dust, ash and gases

Vent – where the magma comes out of the pipe

Volcanic bomb

Crater – bowl-shaped opening around the vent

Pipe – the main channel up the middle of a volcano

Layers of volcanic ash – tiny particles of lava

Dyke – this leads from the pipe to the surface

Magma chamber – place where magma collects below the Earth's crust

Growing

When a volcano erupts, the lava and ash it throws out eventually set as a solid layer of volcanic rock. As the layers build up, the volcano grows. Thick lava flows only a short way before setting, so it forms steep-sided cone volcanoes. Thinner lava flows farther before setting hard, so it forms shield volcanoes that have gently sloping sides.

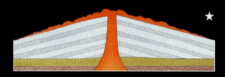

A cross-section through a shield volcano

Bombs and blocks

Volcanic bombs and blocks are thick lumps of molten lava which are blasted into the air as a volcano erupts. They start to cool and harden as they travel through the air. Blocks tend to be angular whereas bombs are more rounded.

Some blocks are the size of trucks.

As they twist through the air, some bombs form a "tail".

Tiny bombs shaped like drops form from very runny lava.

Dead or alive?

Volcanoes that erupt regularly are known as active volcanoes. Volcanoes that won't ever erupt again are called extinct volcanoes. Sometimes, people think a volcano is extinct when actually it is only dormant (sleeping). Volcanoes can lie dormant for thousands of years.

Internet links

To watch video clips of volcanoes erupting and find out more about Pompeii and the eruption of Vesuvius, go to
www.usborne.com/quicklinks

Danger

Lava destroys everything it engulfs but, because it usually flows quite slowly, it rarely kills people. There is more danger from the hot gas, bombs and ash which can sweep down a volcano's slopes at speeds of 200kph (120mph). In AD79, when Mount Vesuvius in Italy erupted, the people of Pompeii were wiped out by poisonous gas and ash.

A plaster cast made from the hollow of a body left in the ash in Pompeii.

Most volcanoes occur at weak spots on the Earth's crust where magma bursts through. Volcanoes erupt in different ways, depending on the thickness of the lava.

Hot spots

Some volcanoes form in the middle of plates. They may be caused by hot zones deep in the Earth's mantle. Scientists think that currents of warm rock called plumes rise slowly through the mantle and make magma which burns through the Earth's crust to make a hot spot volcano.

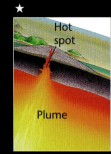

A diagram showing a hot spot volcano in the middle of a plate

Volcanoes with runny lava, like this, erupt gently.

Spreading ridges

Whole mountain ranges of volcanoes can form at underwater boundaries where two plates* are moving apart. These are called spreading ridges. As the plates move apart, magma from the mantle rises to the surface. Most of it solidifies on the edge of the plates to make new crust, but some works its way up to the seabed, where it erupts as volcanoes.

Subduction zones

Volcanoes also occur at subduction zones. These are places where two plates collide head on and one plate is pushed down beneath the other. As the plate is forced deeper and deeper underground, it begins to melt, forming magma. This newly formed magma rises up through cracks in the surface and explodes in a volcano.

Spreading ridges form when plates move apart.
Rising magma

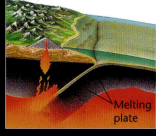

At subduction zones, one plate is forced underground where it starts to melt.
Melting plate

*Plates, 18

Lava

Not all volcanoes erupt in the same way. Some throw clouds of ash high into the air, while others have gentle lava fountains. The thicker and stickier the lava, the more gases are trapped within it. These gases create the pressure which makes a volcano erupt explosively. When lava is thin and runny, gases can escape more easily. They just bubble out of the top of the volcano.

Internet links
To examine different types of volcanoes and build your own online, go to **www.usborne.com/quicklinks**

Hawaiian-type eruptions are usually gentle. They occur when lava is runny, so trapped gases bubble out easily.

Plinian-type eruptions are the most explosive. Trapped gases cause massive explosions as they escape, and huge amounts of volcanic ash are thrown high into the air.

NATURAL HOT WATER

In areas where volcanoes are found, there are often other dramatic natural features. Hot springs, jets of hot water and underwater chimneys that belch out black water can also be caused by volcanic activity.

Internet links

For links to websites with video clips of geysers, black smokers and hot springs, go to www.usborne.com/quicklinks

Hot rock

In volcanic areas, when magma rises into the Earth's crust, it heats the rock around it. This rock might contain groundwater, which is rain or sea water that has seeped down into the Earth's crust through cracks in the surface. As the rock heats up, so does the groundwater around it, producing a natural supply of hot water.

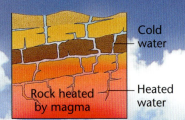

Hot rock heats up groundwater. ★

Hot springs

Groundwater heated by hot rock sometimes bubbles to the surface as a hot, or thermal, spring. The water usually contains minerals which have been dissolved from the rock below. Minerals from the water often build up around the edge of the spring.

This is the Morning Glory pool, one of many hot springs in Yellowstone National Park, USA. The park has over 10,000 features, such as hot springs and geysers, that have been caused by hot, volcanic rock.

*Minerals, 21

Black smokers

Around volcanic mountain ranges under the sea, hot springs sometimes emerge through holes in the seabed called hydrothermal vents.

Some vents, called black smokers, look like chimneys and puff out plumes of hot, cloudy black water. The water is cloudy because of the minerals it has dissolved from the hot rock. As minerals are deposited around the vent, the sides of the chimney build up. Some unusual creatures, such as tubeworms and blind spider crabs, live near black smokers. They feed on bacteria that live on the minerals given out by the vents.

Black smokers form on the seabed and puff out clouds of hot, black water. Some are as tall as 6m (20ft).

Geysers

A geyser is a jet of hot water and steam that shoots into the air from a hole in the ground. Geysers occur when heated groundwater gets trapped in a network of cracks under the Earth's surface. Because the water is trapped, it continues to heat up until it boils and forms steam. The pressure builds up until it forces the water to find a way out of the ground. This results in occasional bursts of hot water.

"Old Faithful" is a geyser in Yellowstone National Park, USA. A fountain of hot water like this spurts out once every hour or so.

VOLCANIC ISLANDS

A volcanic island called White Island, off the coast of New Zealand

If a volcano on the seabed erupts enough times, it may become tall enough to reach the surface of the sea and begin to form an island. As ash and lava from repeated eruptions pile up around the vent, the island grows.

Hot spot islands

Hot spot volcanoes* under the sea sometimes grow into volcanic islands. Over thousands of years, a hot spot can produce a chain of volcanic islands. Scientists think that the rising plume remains in a fixed position inside the Earth's mantle, while the plate above moves. Over a long period of time, a volcanic island is carried away from the plume that caused it.

When an island moves away from a hot spot, the volcano becomes extinct as it loses its supply of magma. A new volcano then forms on the part of the plate lying above the plume. Eventually a chain of islands is formed.

The Hawaiian island chain is made up of hot spot volcanic islands.

*Hot spots, 30

Internet links

For links to websites about hot spot volcanoes and how volcanic islands are formed, go to www.usborne.com/quicklinks

An island is born

This picture shows steam and ash billowing from Surtsey, a volcanic island near Iceland.

In 1963, fishermen off the coast of Iceland saw smoke rising from the sea. They thought it must be a boat on fire. In fact, it wasn't smoke, but ash and steam from a volcano just below the water's surface.

During the next four years, the volcano erupted many times. As it emerged above the water, the eruptions became more explosive as the water pressure decreased. Lava and ash built up, until eventually they formed a volcanic island. The island was named Surtsey after Surt, the Nordic giant of fire.

Black beaches

Some volcanic islands have black sandy beaches. This is because they are formed from basalt lava which is black. When the lava runs down to meet the sea, it cools instantly. The change in temperature makes the lava shatter into tiny pieces which form the grains of sand.

A black sandy beach in Tahiti

LIVING WITH VOLCANOES

Despite the danger that active volcanoes present, many people choose to live on their slopes. Scientists are sometimes able to predict eruptions and warn those at risk.

> **Internet links**
> To watch video clips and see photo galleries of Mount St Helens and other volcanic eruptions, go to www.usborne.com/quicklinks

Monitoring volcanoes

Before a volcano erupts, the ground may change shape. This kind of change can be measured by instruments such as tiltmeters and geodimeters. The ground may also begin to tremble. This is known as volcanic tremor. It can be detected by seismometers.

Such instruments were used to monitor the Mount St. Helens volcano, Washington, USA, in early 1980. They recorded a bulge swelling by 1.5m (5ft) per day. The area around the volcano was evacuated shortly before it erupted.

A group of experts monitoring the Mount St. Helens volcano were in a plane flying over it when the volcano began to shudder. This photograph of the eruption was taken as the pilot turned the plane to escape the blast.

The area around Mount St. Helens after the eruption. Despite the evacuation of the area, 61 people died.

A bulge on the side of Mount St. Helens swelled to 90m (295ft) before a massive eruption blasted away the side of the volcano.

Using volcanoes

Although volcanoes are usually a destructive force, they can also be put to productive uses.

The ash from volcanoes contains minerals which make soil very fertile. As a result, the land around volcanoes is very good for farming. This is one of the reasons why people choose to live in such dangerous places.

Engineers have discovered how to use the heat energy in volcanic rock to produce electricity. When groundwater seeps into the cracks in volcanic rock, it gets hot. (Sometimes cracks are created artificially to produce the same effect.) The hot water is then pumped up to the surface where it is converted into steam. The steam is used to turn machines called turbines which make electricity.

A power station produces electricity.

Hot water is pumped to the surface to turn turbines.

Cold water is pumped into the ground.

Artificial cracks

At some power stations, cold water is pumped into specially-made cracks in volcanic rock.

EARTHQUAKE EFFECTS

An earthquake is a sudden release of energy that makes the ground tremble. The effects of a large earthquake can be devastating: the ground lurches violently and buildings sway from side to side, or may even collapse. However, earthquakes only occur in certain parts of the world and most earthquakes are not felt by people at all.

An apartment block in San Francisco, USA, which has been damaged by an earthquake

Damaging effects

Earthquakes cause most damage when they occur in large towns and cities. During severe earthquakes, buildings and bridges collapse, and cracks called fissures may appear in the ground. There are also threats from hazards such as fire and flooding. These may be caused when underground gas pipes or water pipes crack during an earthquake.

The power of earthquakes

Over 800,000 earthquakes occur each year, but only around a hundred of these cause serious damage. Their power and effects are measured by seismologists, scientists who study earthquakes.

There are two main scales used today for measuring earthquakes: the moment magnitude scale and the Mercalli intensity scale. The moment magnitude scale measures the power of vibrations called seismic waves that travel through the ground when an earthquake happens. These tremors are registered using a device called a seismometer. Then a chart of the vibrations, known as a seismogram, is produced.

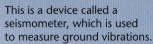

This is a device called a seismometer, which is used to measure ground vibrations.

A survivor views the devastation caused by an earthquake in Sichuan, China, in 2008.

Internet links
For links to websites with video clips, eyewitness accounts and pictures of earthquakes, go to www.usborne.com/quicklinks

Mercalli scale

The Mercalli intensity scale rates earthquakes from I to XII according to the effects of the shaking, including the damage caused in different places. It is based on information from eyewitnesses.

These pictures show how earthquakes are rated in the Mercalli intensity scale. Ratings below IV indicate very slight vibrations.

IV People indoors may notice plates and windows start to rattle.

V Small objects move and liquids in glasses and bowls splash around.

VI Books and ornaments fall off shelves. Vibrations are felt indoors and outdoors.

VII Walls crack and tiles and bricks fall from buildings.

VIII Some weaker buildings collapse.

IX+ Many larger buildings collapse.

HOW EARTHQUAKES HAPPEN

Earthquakes are most common near plate boundaries*. The movement of the plates causes stress to build up in certain areas of rock. When this stress is suddenly released, the surrounding rock vibrates, causing an earthquake.

Fault lines

Earthquakes occur along cracks in the Earth's crust called faults. Faults can be tiny fractures or long cracks stretching over vast distances. They often occur when plates slide against each other, causing the rock to be twisted, stretched or squeezed until it splits. Boundaries where plates slide past each other in the same or in opposite directions are called conservative margins.

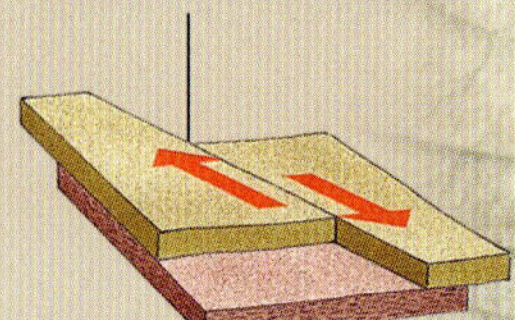

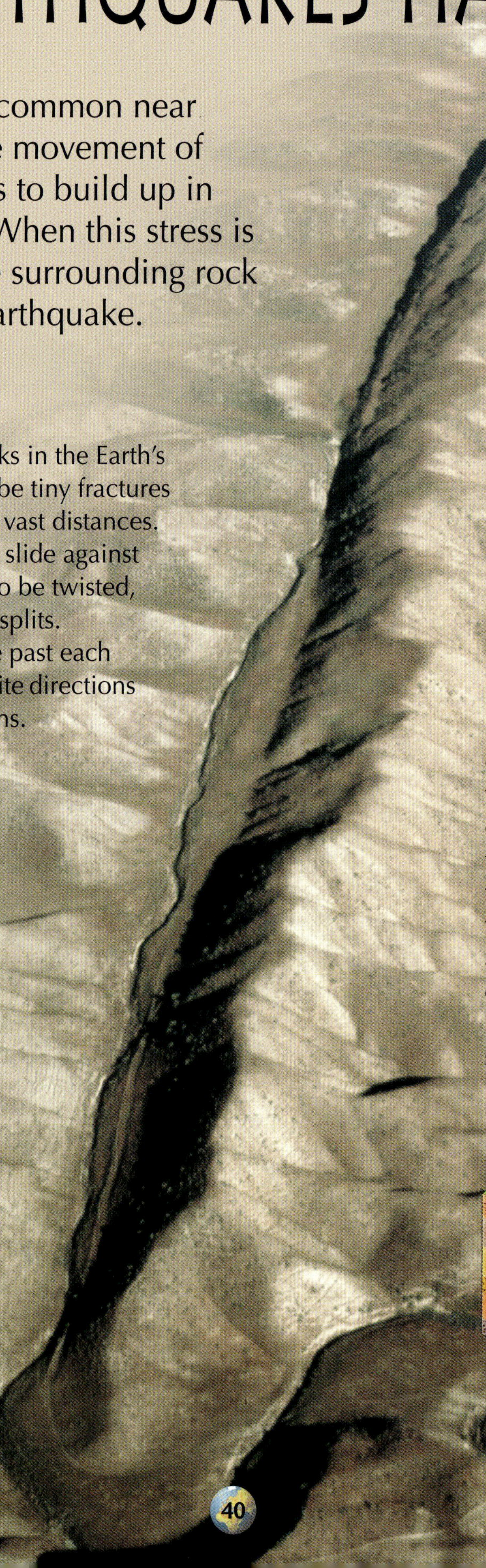

An overhead view of the San Andreas fault

San Francisco • The North American plate moves 1cm (0.4in) a year.
San Andreas fault
The Pacific plate moves 6cm (2.4in) a year.
Los Angeles
San Diego

Earthquakes regularly occur along the San Andreas fault, on the west coast of North America. These plates slide in the same direction, but move at different speeds.

This diagram shows how some plates slide past each other in opposite directions.

Releasing energy

If the jagged edges along a fault become jammed, energy builds up as the two edges strain against one another. Eventually, the stress becomes so great that one side is suddenly forced to give way, causing a jerking movement. The energy that has built up is released, making the surrounding rock vibrate in an earthquake.

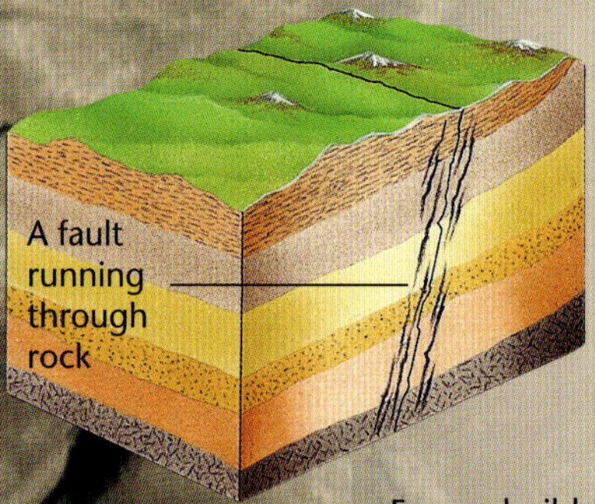

A fault running through rock

Energy builds up at the point where the rocks become jammed.

*Plate boundaries, 18

The focus

The point where the rock gives way is called the focus. This is where the earthquake starts, usually about 5–15km (3–9 miles) underground. The point on the surface directly above the focus is called the epicentre*.

Internet links
For links to websites where you can see how earthquakes happen and find out more about California's San Andreas Fault, go to www.usborne.com/quicklinks

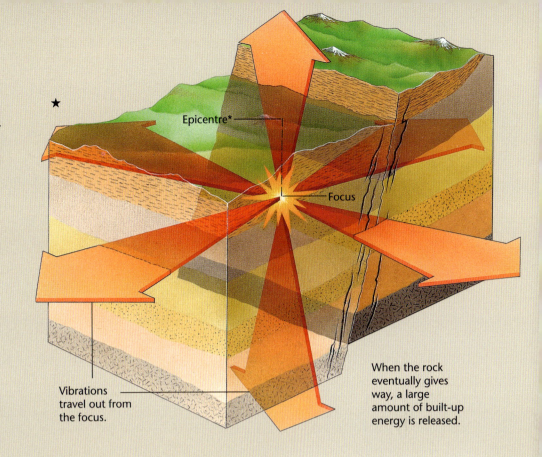

Vibrations travel out from the focus.

When the rock eventually gives way, a large amount of built-up energy is released.

Seismic waves

Seismic waves are at their strongest nearest the focus and become weaker as they travel out. There are different types of seismic waves, each of which makes the rock it travels through vibrate in a different way.

Different types of seismic waves travel by distorting rock in different ways.

→ Direction of waves
↔ Vibrations of the rock particles as the waves pass through

1. P-waves ('P' stands for either primary or push and pull) travel deep below the ground. As they travel through rock, they stretch and squeeze the rock particles.

Stretching and squeezing movement

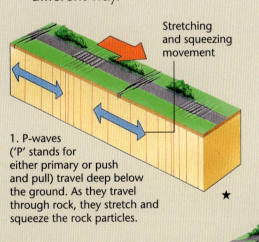

2. S-waves ('S' stands for secondary or shake) make rock move up and down and from side to side. They travel deep underground and can't move through liquid.

Vertical and horizontal movement

3. L-waves ('L' stands for long) only travel along the surface. Most earthquake damage is caused by this type of wave.

Circular movement

Aftershocks

Sometimes, not all of the energy that has built up is released during an earthquake. This may mean that after the main earthquake there are smaller tremors, known as aftershocks, as the remaining energy is released. Small amounts of energy may also be released before an earthquake occurs. This produces tremors known as foreshocks.

*Epicenter (USA)

EARTHQUAKE SAFETY

By monitoring faults, scientists can sometimes predict when and where earthquakes are likely to occur. This means that they can take steps to limit the damage caused by an earthquake or even prevent an earthquake from happening.

Seismic gaps

Stress that builds up at fault boundaries is often released gradually by slow movement known as fault creep. Earthquakes are less likely to happen in areas where fault creep occurs, because stress is being released. They are most likely to occur at sections of a fault where there has been no movement for many years. These sections are known as seismic gaps.

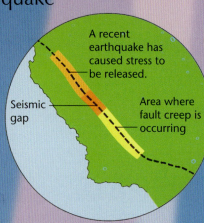

By identifying seismic gaps, scientists can carefully monitor areas where earthquakes are most likely to occur.

Monitoring faults

If the surface of the Earth suddenly starts to tilt, it may be a sign that an earthquake is about to happen. Devices called tiltmeters can measure tiny changes in the level of the ground. Horizontal movement along faults can be monitored using lasers. A laser beam from one side of the fault is bounced off a reflector on the other side, which reflects it back. A computer records the time it takes the beam to travel this distance. If the time changes, it shows that movement has taken place.

Scientists use lasers like these to detect ground movements. They can detect shifts as slight as 1mm (0.04in).

Preventing earthquakes

Earthquakes can be prevented by releasing jammed plates before too much stress builds up. This can be done by conducting a small explosion to shift the plates. Alternatively, drilling deep holes and injecting water into rocks reduces friction, enabling smoother movement along a fault.

Keeping safe

During an earthquake, if you are indoors, the safest place to be is under a solid table or desk. You should cover your eyes to protect them from flying glass and hold on tightly to the leg of the table. If you are outside, it's better to be in an open space, away from buildings, trees and power lines.

Internet links

For links to websites where you can find fascinating earthquake facts, pictures and animations, and discover how to stay safe during an earthquake, go to www.usborne.com/quicklinks

Safe buildings

In areas where there is a high risk of earthquakes happening, more buildings are being designed so that minimum damage is caused if there is an earthquake. The foundations of some buildings are constructed to absorb vibrations and reduce the effects of shaking. Steel frames can be used to strengthen buildings, so that a building may sway but will not collapse when the ground trembles.

The Transamerica skyscraper in San Francisco, USA, is designed to withstand tremors.

Animal instincts

Scientists think that animals' highly developed senses may alert them to earthquakes before they happen. It is possible that they can detect slight vibrations, changes in electrical currents in rocks, or the release of gases. In San Francisco, USA, zoo animals are monitored in case the way they behave gives warning of an earthquake.

If animals become unusually agitated, it may be a clue that an earthquake is about to happen.

GIANT WAVES

An earthquake or a volcanic eruption under the sea or near the coast can cause giant waves called tsunami. These waves surge across the sea in all directions. Just before a tsunami crashes onto the shore, it may swell to an enormous height.

This photograph shows some of the terrible devastation caused by the Indian Ocean Tsunami of 2004 in Tamil Nadu, India.

Tsunami

Tsunami begin when an earthquake or volcano causes the water to shift and waves to form. Out at sea, tsunami are a similar height to ordinary waves, but the distance between one tsunami and the next can be more than 100km (62 miles). What makes tsunami so dangerous is their speed. They race across the sea at speeds of up to 800kph (500mph). Normally tsunami do not break like ordinary waves. As a tsunami enters shallow water, its height increases and it surges over the land. This is what causes the devastating flooding of coastal regions.

Internet links

For links to websites where you can watch video clips about how tsunami form and find out more about tsunami warning systems in the Pacific Ocean, go to www.usborne.com/quicklinks

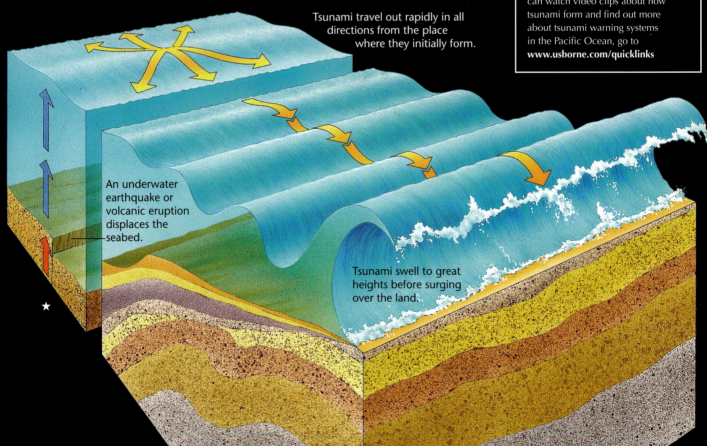

Tsunami travel out rapidly in all directions from the place where they initially form.

An underwater earthquake or volcanic eruption displaces the seabed.

Tsunami swell to great heights before surging over the land.

Tsunami warning system

Most tsunami occur in the Pacific Ocean. For this reason, there are observation stations throughout the Pacific to monitor earthquakes. If an earthquake is large enough to generate tsunami, warnings are issued to coastal towns, so that they can prepare for it. Tide stations along the coast then monitor the arrival of the tsunami.

Observation and tide stations in the Pacific monitor tsunami.

Tsunami look like a huge wall of water. They can reach heights of up to 50m (165ft).

Autumn in the Cache National Forest, Idaho, USA

CLIMATE

THE EARTH'S ATMOSPHERE

Surrounding the Earth is a blanket of gases which makes up its atmosphere. The atmosphere contains the air we need to breathe. It also affects weather and climate and protects us from extremes of temperature and from the Sun's harmful rays.

The atmosphere's structure

The gases surrounding the Earth are held by its gravity, a force which attracts things to Earth. The atmosphere is divided into layers according to the temperature of these gases. The diagram below shows the different layers.

This diagram shows some of the layers in the Earth's atmosphere. The outermost layer, the exosphere, is not marked; it is around 500km (310 miles) from Earth.

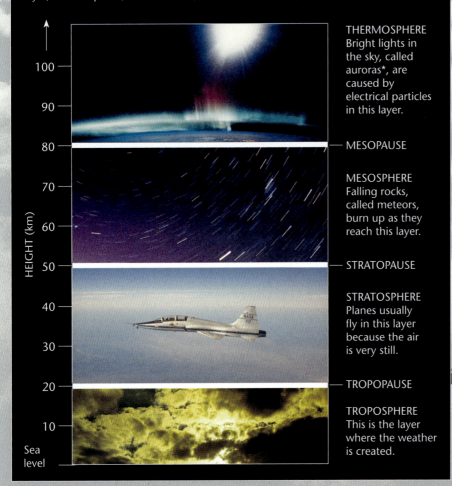

THERMOSPHERE
Bright lights in the sky, called auroras*, are caused by electrical particles in this layer.

MESOPAUSE

MESOSPHERE
Falling rocks, called meteors, burn up as they reach this layer.

STRATOPAUSE

STRATOSPHERE
Planes usually fly in this layer because the air is very still.

TROPOPAUSE

TROPOSPHERE
This is the layer where the weather is created.

The troposphere

The troposphere is the layer of the atmosphere nearest to the Earth's surface. As well as a mixture of gases, this layer contains clouds, dust and pollution. It extends to between 10km (6 miles) and 20km (12 miles) from the Earth. Temperatures are high near the Earth because the air is heated from below by the Earth's surface, which is warmed by the Sun. Higher up, the air is thinner and can't hold as much heat, so temperatures decrease.

The troposphere is the layer where the weather is produced. It gets its name from the Greek word *tropos* which means "a turn". This is because the air there is constantly circulating*.

*Air currents, 50; auroras, 90

The stratosphere

The upper limit of the stratosphere is around 50km (30 miles) from the Earth's surface. The stratosphere contains a concentration of ozone gas. This layer of ozone gas is very important, as it absorbs ultraviolet rays from the Sun which can cause skin cancer.

The mesosphere

The mesosphere reaches to a height of around 80km (50 miles). Temperatures there are the coolest in the atmosphere because there is very little ozone, dust or clouds to absorb energy from the Sun. It is warmer at the bottom as there is more ozone there.

Internet links

To find out more about the Earth's atmosphere and the status of the ozone layer over Antarctica, go to www.usborne.com/quicklinks

The thermosphere

Temperatures in the thermosphere can be extremely high, reaching up to 1,500°C (2,732°F). This is because there is a high proportion of a gas called atomic oxygen. This gets warmed as it absorbs energy from the Sun.

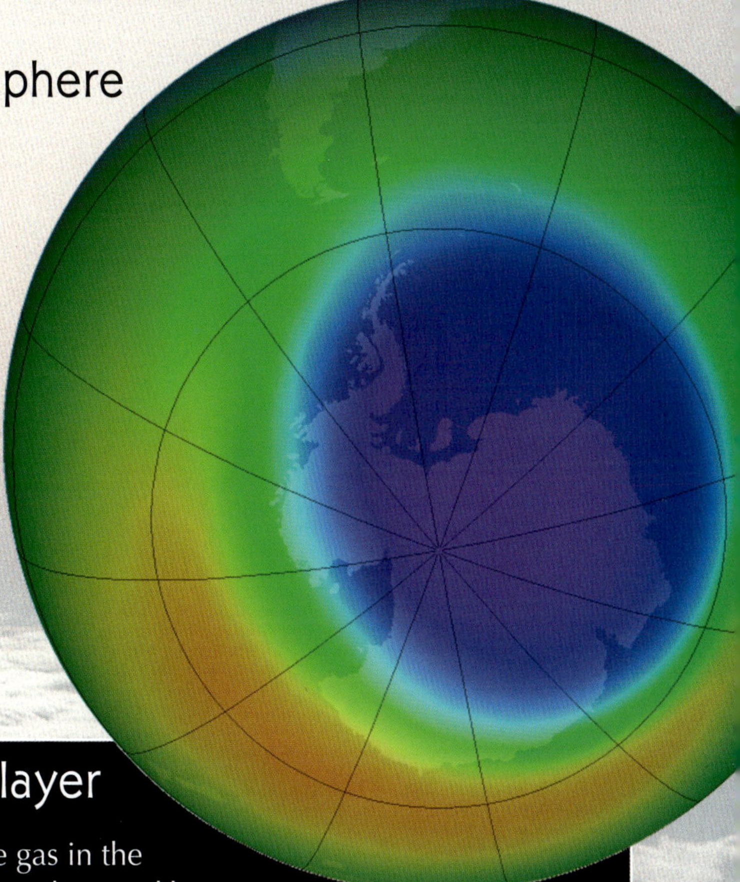

The ozone layer

The layer of ozone gas in the stratosphere is being damaged by chemicals called chlorofluorocarbons (CFCs), which are used in some spray cans and refrigerators. At certain times of year, a hole in the ozone layer appears over Antarctica, and in other areas the ozone layer becomes very thin. This damage means that more of the Sun's harmful ultraviolet rays reach the Earth's surface.

The deep purple area in this picture shows a hole in the layer of ozone gas over Antarctica.

When you fly in a plane in the stratosphere you can often see the clouds in the troposphere below.

AIR AND OCEAN CURRENTS

As the Sun heats the Earth, it causes air and water to move around in the form of currents. As particles of air and water are heated, they first expand and rise and then they cool and fall, producing patterns of circulating air and water, which are crucial in determining climate.

The circular shapes on the satellite image in the background are called spiral eddies. They are swirls of water that have separated from the main band, or current, of water.

Moving air

The air around us is constantly pushing in every direction. The force that it exerts is known as atmospheric pressure.

The movement of air is affected by temperature. The Sun heats up the land and oceans, which in turn heat the air directly above in the troposphere*. As the air is heated, it rises and so leaves behind an area of low pressure. When the air cools, it sinks down on the Earth's surface in a different area, causing high pressure.

Because the Sun doesn't heat up the world evenly, there are differences of pressure. Where there is a difference, air flows from high to low pressure areas in order to even out the pressure. This moving air is wind. As the air moves, the spinning of the Earth causes it to be deflected sideways. This deflection is known as the Coriolis effect*.

Global winds

Air is constantly circulating between the tropics and the poles as global winds. Warm air flows from the tropics and displaces the cold air at the poles, which then flows back toward the tropics. Global winds form because areas near the Equator receive more heat from the Sun than other areas. As the air is heated, it rises and spreads out. When it cools, it sinks at around 30° north and south of the Equator. This increases pressure at the Earth's surface and air at the base of the atmosphere is forced outward in the direction of both the Equator and the poles. The surface air currents moving toward the Equator are called the trade winds.

A satellite image showing winds over the Pacific Ocean. The tiny arrows overlaying the image show the direction of the winds.

*Coriolis effect, 84; tropics, 146; troposphere, 48

Moving water

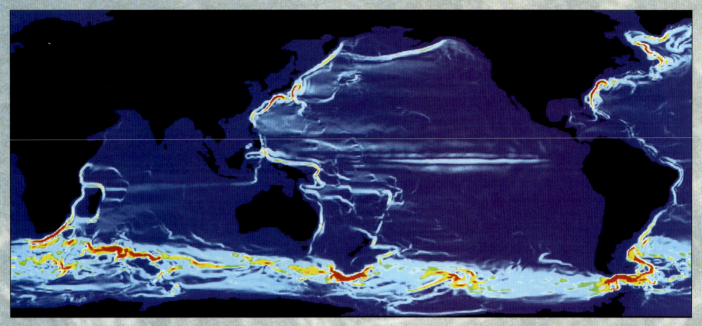

This image shows ocean currents around the world. The red areas are fast currents and the light blue areas are slow currents.

Ocean currents are wide bands of water, like rivers that flow in the world's oceans. They sweep around the oceans, moving water between hot and cold places.

Heat from the Sun also causes the movement of water in the form of currents. However, in the oceans, the temperature difference between the poles and the Equator is greater than it is on land. Near the Equator, the Sun's rays penetrate far below the ocean's surface. At the poles, the Sun's rays hit the water at a shallow angle. This causes the water to act like a mirror, reflecting rather than absorbing the Sun's rays.

Internet links
To watch video clips and examine diagrams about different air and ocean currents, and to investigate how El Niño can affect weather around the world, go to **www.usborne.com/quicklinks**

Effects of currents

Currents vary in temperature and move at different speeds. If a current is much warmer or cooler than the surrounding water, it can dramatically affect the climates of the nearby coastal areas. A warm current called the Gulf Stream, which runs between the Gulf of Mexico and Europe, brings a mild climate to northwest Europe.

El Niño

The incredible effect that the warming of the ocean can have on weather and climate is illustrated by a phenomenon known as El Niño. Every few years, a current of water in the Pacific, off the northwest coast of South America, suddenly becomes warmer. Scientists are not sure why it happens, but it causes a chain of climatic changes around the world, including floods and severe storms.

A satellite picture of part of the Gulf Stream, a current of warm water that flows in the Atlantic Ocean

NATURAL CYCLES

Some substances, such as nitrogen and carbon, are constantly changing form as they move around in huge cycles. This exchange of substances is essential to life on Earth. The air, land, water, plants, animals, and even your own body, all form a part of these cycles.

This magnified part of a pea plant contains bacteria which convert nitrogen from the air into a form the plant can use.

Keeping a balance

Living things take in substances such as oxygen, nitrogen, carbon and water from the world around them through food, soil and air. They use them to live and grow. When a plant or animal dies and decays, its body is broken down and gases are released into the air. The cycle continues, with these substances being used again and again. This process maintains the balance of gases in the air.

The nitrogen cycle

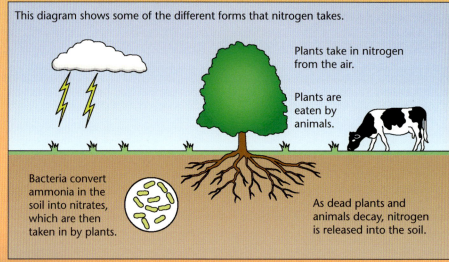

This diagram shows some of the different forms that nitrogen takes.

Plants take in nitrogen from the air.

Plants are eaten by animals.

Bacteria convert ammonia in the soil into nitrates, which are then taken in by plants.

As dead plants and animals decay, nitrogen is released into the soil.

Nitrogen (chemical symbol – N) makes up 78% of the air. Plants and animals need it for growth. Plants take in nitrogen from the air and the soil. Bacteria convert the substance into a form the plants can use. Animals obtain nitrogen by eating plants or by eating animals that have eaten plants. When plants and animals die and decay, fungi and bacteria break down their remains and nitrogen is released back into the soil.

This dung beetle is feeding on animal dung. Insects like this help to break down plant and animal matter.

One form that carbon can take is charcoal, as shown here. Charcoal can be burned as a fuel. When it is burned, it gives out carbon dioxide.

The carbon cycle

Carbon forms part of the gases in the air, mainly as carbon dioxide (chemical symbol – CO_2), which is a compound of carbon and oxygen. Plants take in CO_2 from the air and use it to make food. At night, they give out CO_2.

Animals obtain carbon by eating plants. They release carbon in their waste and when they breathe out. CO_2 is also released when plants and animals die and decay. Carbon can be stored in the form of fossilized remains. Eventually these form fossil fuels* such as coal and oil, which release CO_2 when burned.

Upsetting cycles

Left alone, these cycles create a natural balance of gases. However, human activities interfere with this balance by adding waste and pollution to the atmosphere. The effects of human disruption on the carbon cycle are described on pages 102 to 103.

When farmers harvest crops, they break the nitrogen cycle because the plants are not allowed to decay naturally. Farmers often use a chemical fertilizer* to replace nitrates in soil. If too much is added, it can seep through the soil into rivers, where it can affect plants and animals.

The algae in this canal are thriving because of excess nitrates running into the canal from fertilizer used on nearby farmland.

This diagram shows some of the different forms that carbon takes.

Plants take in carbon dioxide from the air to help them make food. At night, they give out carbon dioxide.

When fossil fuels are burned, carbon dioxide is released.

When dead plants and animals decay, carbon dioxide is released into the air.

Animals take in carbon when they eat plants. They breathe out carbon dioxide.

Internet links

To watch video clips about the importance of the nitrogen and carbon cycles, go to **www.usborne.com/quicklinks**

*Fertilizer, 114; fossil fuels, 24

GLOBAL WARMING

Some of the gases in the atmosphere help to keep the Earth warm. They trap heat from the Sun in the same way that a greenhouse traps heat. This process is known as the greenhouse effect. But, as these gases increase, the Earth might be getting too warm.

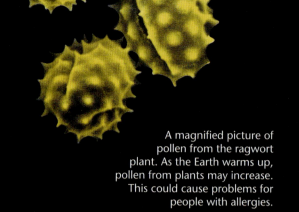

A magnified picture of pollen from the ragwort plant. As the Earth warms up, pollen from plants may increase. This could cause problems for people with allergies.

Greenhouse gases

The Earth's surface absorbs much of the heat from the Sun. This is then given off as heat energy into the atmosphere. It gets trapped there by gases, such as carbon dioxide, which are known as greenhouse gases. As the amount of greenhouse gases increases, more heat is trapped.

Most greenhouse gases occur naturally, but industrial processes and other pollution are increasing the amount of greenhouse gases in the atmosphere. Scientists think that this may be causing the Earth to become warmer. This process is known as global warming.

Plants are important for the balance of greenhouse gases because they take in carbon dioxide.

Balance of gases

Whenever we burn oil, coal or wood, carbon dioxide is released. For example, when forests are burned to make room for farming, they release carbon dioxide. This also reduces the number of plants available to absorb carbon dioxide, upsetting the natural balance of the carbon cycle*. Factories, power stations and cars also give out pollution which may contribute to global warming.

Huge roads, like this one, are useful for car drivers, but the pollution from cars could be contributing to global warming.

Venice, Italy, is a city built on over 100 tiny islands in the Lagoon of Venice. If the sea level rises, it may eventually disappear under the sea.

Rising sea level

As atmospheric temperatures rise, so does the sea level. This will eventually result in the flooding of low-lying areas. Scientists estimate that the sea level is rising at a rate of about 3mm (0.12in) each year. It may rise by another 0.5–1m (1.6–3.3ft) by the year 2100. There are two main reasons for the increased volume of water. First, as the oceans heat up, the water expands. The sea level rises because the water takes up more space. Secondly, the higher temperatures may cause glaciers and icecaps on land to melt. This water will then flood into the sea.

Changing climate

Scientists predict the average atmospheric temperature will increase by 1.4–4.8°C (2.4–8.6°F) this century. Extreme weather may become more common. Climate change will affect the habitats* of plants and animals. Some species may thrive, but others may struggle to survive.

Internet links

For links to websites where you can find out more about global warming and how it may affect sea levels and contribute to climate change, go to www.usborne.com/quicklinks

Shifting the balance

People have already begun to take steps to reduce the emission of gases that contribute to global warming. The main ways that this can be achieved are by looking at alternative energy sources and reducing pollution levels.

*Carbon cycle, 53; habitats, 100

WORLD CLIMATES

The long-term or typical pattern of weather in a particular area is known as its climate. Climates vary enormously in different parts of the world. They determine the character of an area, affecting the plants, animals and people that live there.

This map of the Earth's surface contains information from several different satellites*. It shows some of the main climate types around the world.

Maple trees grow in temperate regions.

 Temperate and tropical regions are green. They contain lots of vegetation.

 Tropical grasslands and deserts are yellow and brown. They are dry, with little vegetation.

 Snowy regions are light blue or white. The swirling white masses are clouds.

Climate types

Areas can be grouped into several main climate types, such as polar, temperate and tropical. These are also known as biomes*. The most important factor in determining an area's climate is its latitude*, because this affects the amount of heat received from the Sun. This in turn has a crucial effect on the vegetation and animals which give each climate zone its distinctive characteristics.

The map above shows how areas at the same latitude share broadly similar climates. The different climate zones are described in more detail on the following pages.

Other factors, such as height and distance from the ocean, are also very important in determining the climate of a particular area.

*Biomes, 101; latitude, 10; satellites, 11

High places

Mountain regions have a different climate from the surrounding lowland areas. It rains and snows frequently, as the mountains force clouds to rise higher. Temperatures can be extremely cold because mountain air is thinner and can't hold as much heat.

Internet links

For links to websites where you can learn about the different climates around the world, go to www.usborne.com/quicklinks

Moose live in forests in cool temperate regions.

Land and sea

Climate is affected by the oceans. Places near the sea have a maritime climate, a milder and wetter climate than areas farther inland. Temperatures there are not usually so extreme as inland areas at the same latitude. This is because ocean temperatures change less than land temperatures and this affects the climate of areas nearby. The climates of inland areas are known as continental climates.

Land surfaces

Different land surfaces absorb the Sun's rays differently. Light surfaces, such as snow-covered land or deserts, reflect the Sun's rays, whereas dense forests and dark soils absorb them. Where a higher proportion of the rays is reflected, clouds are less likely to form. This means that areas with lighter land surfaces will have less rainfall. Clouds also reflect the Sun's rays, affecting the amount of energy reaching the Earth's surface.

RAINFORESTS

In the tropics*, it rains nearly every day and is hot throughout the year. Large areas are covered in thick, lush forests called tropical rainforests.

Rainy places

Tropical rainforests receive more than 2,000mm (80in) of rain each year. The intense heat causes water to evaporate quickly, making the air very moist, or humid.

> **Internet links**
> For links to websites where you can discover more about the world's rainforests and why these regions are under threat, go to www.usborne.com/quicklinks

This is a tropical rainforest in Bali, Indonesia. The trees grow quickly as they compete to reach the light.

Rainforest trees spread out their branches to absorb the light, forming a canopy which can be up to 7m (23ft) thick.

This map shows where the tropical rainforests are.

*Tropics, 146

Rainforest people

Many small ethnic groups living in tropical rainforests survive by hunting animals and gathering plants, or by small-scale farming. However, their lifestyle has been threatened by people who have moved to these areas for commercial reasons. They chop down trees and burn them in order to clear land for farming and mining.

These rainforest trees are being burned to create space for farming.

Animal life

Rainforests are home to over half the world's plant and animal species. Different kinds of animals have adapted to living at different levels in the rainforest. Many animals live in the branches of trees. They need to be good at climbing and able to move easily from tree to tree by swinging, jumping or gliding.

On the forest floor, it is dark and the tangled vegetation makes it difficult for some animals to move around. The larger animals tend to be sturdy so they can easily force their way through. There are also many insects.

Colugos climb trees for food. They use the flaps of skin between their arms and legs to help them glide between trees.

Forests in danger

Every year, huge areas of rainforest are chopped down or burned. The disappearance of so many trees affects the balance of gases in the atmosphere. This may cause an increase in global warming*. Due to the destruction of their natural habitat, many rainforest plants and animals have died out and many others are endangered.

Golden lion tamarins are an endangered species of monkey.

*Global warming, 54

TROPICAL GRASSLANDS

The tropical grasslands are flat, open plains in the central parts of continents. They occur between 5° and 15° north and south of the Equator and get their name from the grasses that make up the majority of their vegetation.

This map shows where the tropical grasslands are.

Two seasons

The tropical grasslands have two seasons: a dry season, when the vegetation is dry and brown, and a rainy season, when the grasses become tall and green.

The rainy season occurs when the Sun is directly overhead and the trade winds* meet and cause rainfall. As the Sun moves, so does the point where the trade winds meet until the dry season begins.

Vegetation

Only a few trees grow in the tropical grasslands, for example the acacia tree whose thick trunk is resistant to the fires that sometimes rage during the dry season. However, there are around 8,000 species of grasses, which are suited to dry conditions. They have long roots which can reach downward and sideways in search of water.

Acacia trees in the Taragire National Park, Tanzania, Africa. Acacias are among the few trees that can survive in the dry tropical grasslands.

Internet links

For links to websites where you can watch some of the most amazing animals of the tropical grasslands, go to www.usborne.com/quicklinks

*Trade winds, 50

Grassland animals

The tropical grasslands are home to large numbers of herbivores (plant-eating animals). These attract large hunting animals, such as lions and cheetahs, that feed on them. Because the land is so exposed, many animals live in large groups, so that some animals can watch out for predators while others feed or rest.

Some of the fastest animals, such as cheetahs, gazelles and ostriches, live in grasslands. Speed is important for survival, both for the hunters and the hunted. With so few hiding places, a hunt for food often results in a chase.

During the dry season, wildebeest move away, or migrate, to find food and water. Many thousands of wildebeest migrate together for protection.

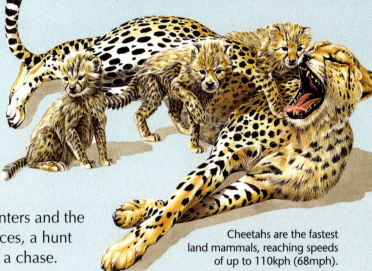

Cheetahs are the fastest land mammals, reaching speeds of up to 110kph (68mph).

The tsetse fly

Many grassland areas are now used for farming. However, the largest grasslands, in Africa, are almost untouched. This is because of a parasite, carried by an insect called the tsetse fly, which infects humans and animals. In humans, it causes sleeping sickness, the effects of which are sluggishness, fever and sometimes death. In animals, it causes a similar disease called nagana.

A close-up of a tsetse fly feeding on a human arm

MONSOONS

At certain times of year, some areas of the tropics have a period of torrential rain and another period of drier weather. This strong seasonal change is known as a monsoon. The rain can cause severe flooding, but people also rely on it for survival.

Three seasons

Monsoons occur in certain parts of the tropics, particularly in Southeast Asia. Monsoon regions have three seasons – a long, cool dry season, a hot humid season when the land is very dry and a rainy season when there are thunderstorms on most days.

During the rainy season, it rains very heavily and there are strong winds. You can see how strong the winds are by the way the trees are blowing.

Changing winds

The word *monsoon* is from an Arabic word meaning "season". It refers to the seasonal reversal of the wind direction. During the cooler season, the land is cooler than the ocean, and so winds blow from the land to the ocean, giving dry weather over the land. The warm season occurs when the midday Sun is almost directly overhead. The land is hotter than the ocean, so moist winds rush in from the ocean and shed their moisture on the land as heavy rain.

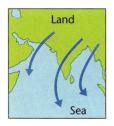 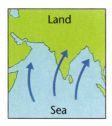

In the dry season, winds blow from the land to the sea.

In the rainy season, moist winds rush in from the sea.

Farming

Around a quarter of the world's people live in monsoon areas. Many of them rely on growing their own food. The main crops are rice and tea, which grow well in wet conditions.

Rice in particular needs lots of water to grow. The seedlings are planted during the wet monsoon season in flooded fields called paddy fields. Rice is an important food for many poor nations, because it can be grown cheaply and in large quantities. If there is too little rain, it can be disastrous, resulting in crop failure which may in turn cause famine.

> **Internet links**
>
> For links to websites where you can find out more about monsoons and see how they affect people's lives, go to www.usborne.com/quicklinks

A rice farm in China. The field has been flooded with water, as rice plants grow well in waterlogged soils.

Diseases

A mosquito magnified. These insects thrive in monsoon regions.

A number of serious diseases spread easily after the monsoon season, because stagnant floodwater provides an ideal breeding ground for the bacteria that cause them. Typhoid and cholera are particularly common. Mosquitoes, insects which can carry diseases such as malaria and yellow fever, also thrive in the warm, wet conditions of monsoon regions.

*Soil erosion, 115

TROPICAL DESERTS

The tropical deserts are the hottest and driest places in the world. With so little water or shelter, only a few animals and plants are able to survive in the burning heat of the day. Very few people live in tropical deserts.

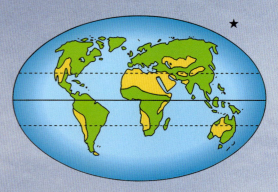

Tropical deserts exist mainly between 15° and 30° north and south of the Equator.

This is a fertile area, called an oasis, in the Thar Desert, Rajasthan, India. The people are collecting water.

Desert climate

Most deserts are hot during the day and cold at night. During the day, the heat is intense because the Sun is high in the sky and there are few clouds to block the Sun's rays. Temperatures can reach over 52°C (126°F). At night, the lack of clouds allows heat to escape, so temperatures can drop to below freezing. Less than 250mm (10in) of rain falls on deserts each year. When it rains, it is usually in short, violent storms. If the land has been baked by the heat of the Sun, these brief rainstorms can cause floods because the rain is not absorbed quickly enough by the dry ground.

Oases

There is water in the desert, but most of it is located underground in rocks that are porous, which means they can hold water like a sponge. In a few places, where these rocks are at the surface, moist areas called oases are formed. Birds, animals and people gather at oases to drink.

*Porous rocks, 128

Desert landscapes

Only 25% of the world's deserts are sandy. Most deserts consist of bare rock or stone. Some even have dramatic rocky mountains. In sandy deserts, sand often collects together to form hills called dunes, which move and change shape as the wind blows the sand across the desert.

Strong winds sometimes sweep across deserts, causing sand-storms which can wear away the rocks in their path. Over many years, this sand-blasting effect can produce some unusually-shaped rocks. The process of wearing away rocks in this way is a type of erosion*.

This is a sand dune in the Sahara Desert, Africa, the biggest desert in the world. The man is one of the Tuareg, a group of people who live in the Sahara.

Internet links

For links to websites where you can explore the hottest and driest places in the world and find out about the animals and plants that live there, go to www.usborne.com/quicklinks

Adaptation

In order to survive in the desert, those plants and animals that live there have adapted so that they are able to cope with the heat and limited supplies of water. Some desert plants can store water in their stems or can access water deep in the ground through long roots. Many desert animals have dry droppings to help them save water.

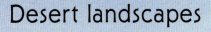

Camels can drink gallons of water in a few minutes and then last days without any.

Desert expansion

The world's deserts are increasing in size. This process, known as desertification, is caused by the destruction of the vegetation near the edges of deserts. People living in these dry areas need grass for their animals to eat and wood from trees to burn as fuel. This destruction of vegetation means that the soil is easily washed or blown away and the water cycle* is disrupted. Once this has happened, it is very difficult for vegetation to grow there.

*Erosion, 118; water cycle, 80

MEDITERRANEAN CLIMATES

Mediterranean climates are warm temperate* climates. They get their name from the regions bordering the Mediterranean Sea. However, other parts of the world, such as small areas around Cape Town (South Africa), Perth (Australia), San Francisco (USA) and Valparaiso (Chile) also have Mediterranean climates.

This map shows those areas with a Mediterranean climate.

Warm and dry

Mediterranean climates cover only a small part of the world. They are found on the west coasts of continents between 30° and 40° north and south of the Equator.

In summer in the Mediterranean, descending air usually causes hot, cloudless weather. In winter, the westerly winds bring moist air from the Atlantic, causing wetter weather.

In the Mediterranean region itself, the Mediterranean Sea (an inland sea with a narrow link to the Atlantic Ocean) has a moderating influence on the climate of the surrounding countries, making the winters milder than they would be otherwise.

In other parts of the world that have Mediterranean climates, cold offshore currents* have a similar effect on the local climate as the Mediterranean Sea has on southern Europe.

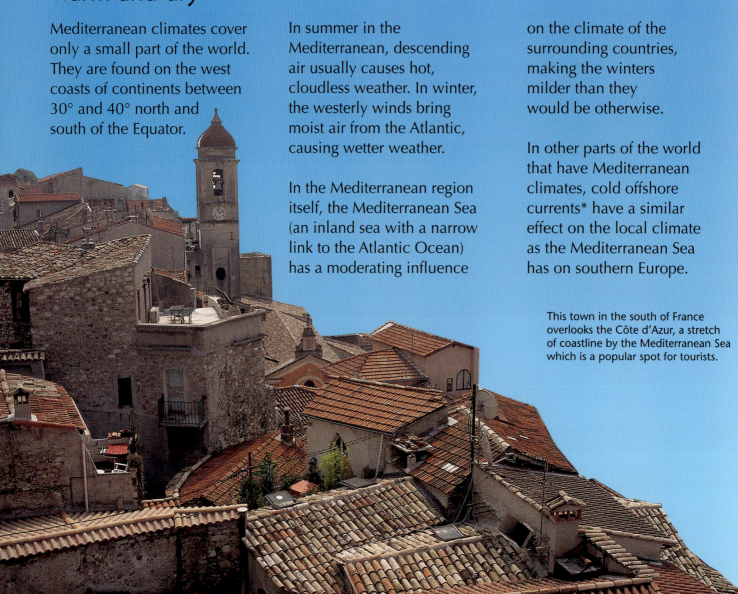

This town in the south of France overlooks the Côte d'Azur, a stretch of coastline by the Mediterranean Sea which is a popular spot for tourists.

Oranges grow well in Mediterranean climates.

Vegetation

There are two main types of vegetation in Mediterranean regions: trees such as cork oaks and olives, and low woody plants, or scrub. The vegetation is well adapted to the dry summer climate. Plants have thick, waxy leaves which reduce the amount of water they lose, and long roots which enable them to reach water deep underground.

Farming

Those places with Mediterranean climates are home to some of the world's most important wine producers. Grape vines are particularly well adapted to the climate, as they have long roots and tough bark.

The Mediterranean climate is also good for growing citrus fruits, such as oranges and lemons. These have thick skins which help them to retain moisture and the hot summers help the fruit to ripen quickly.

Tourism

People sunbathing on a beach in the Côte d'Azur, southern France

The hot, dry summers in Mediterranean countries such as Greece, Spain, Italy and southern France have made them popular destinations for tourists from cooler climates searching for summer sunshine. This has meant that tourism has become an important part of the economies of these countries. Resorts tend to be developed in strips along the coast, where closeness to the sea and pleasant beaches are also major attractions for people.

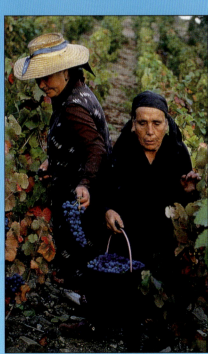

A vineyard in the Douro Valley, Portugal. The grapes are being hand-picked to make wine.

Internet links

For links to websites where you can find out more about Mediterranean climates and the types of crops that thrive in this region including citrus fruits and grapes, go to **www.usborne.com/quicklinks**

67

*Ocean currents, 51; temperate, 68; tropics, 146

TEMPERATE CLIMATES

The areas of the globe between the Arctic and Antarctic Circles and the tropics have a temperate climate. As the term temperate suggests, temperatures there are never very extreme. This vast area contains a wide range of landscapes.

The dark blue areas of this map show the parts of the world with temperate climates.

Varied climates

The vegetation in temperate regions ranges from forests to dry grasslands. However, all the different areas have four seasons*: spring, summer, autumn and winter. This is because of the Earth's tilt and the way that each hemisphere faces the Sun in one season and then faces away from it in another.

Green lands

The mid-latitudes (between 40° and 60° north and south of the Equator) have a rainy climate, which is usually described as cool temperate. The steady rain throughout the year is the result of cool air from the poles meeting warm air from the tropics. The warm air is forced upward, causing swirling patterns of clouds and rain known as depressions.

The moderate temperatures in cool temperate regions mean that vegetation has a long period of uninterrupted growth, so the landscape is very green. Most trees are deciduous, which means that they lose their leaves in winter.

This region, which includes most of Europe, contains the richest farmland areas. The fertile soil and rainfall throughout the year make it suitable for a wide variety of crops, including grains, green vegetables and deciduous fruits.

Before the leaves on deciduous trees fall, they change from green to orange, red and yellow.

*Seasons, 142; tropics, 146

Grasslands

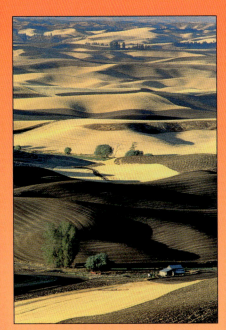

A view of the huge grasslands, or prairies, of North America

The prairies of North America and the steppes of Russia are huge temperate grasslands which lie in the middle of continents. Their summers are hot and sunny, but their winters can be quite harsh because they are away from the warming effects of the ocean*.

These areas receive too little rainfall for trees to grow, so the main vegetation is grasses. In the vast, treeless prairies of North America, winter frosts break up the rich soils, but summer days are long and warm. Wheat is suited to these conditions and is grown extensively.

*Maritime climates, 57

Seasonal life

The lives of many animals and plants in temperate regions follow the cycle of the seasons. Annual plants complete their life's cycle in a year. They begin growing from seeds in spring and then flower in summer. In autumn, they produce their own seeds and fruit. At the end of the year the plants die.

> **Internet links**
> To take a virtual walk in a temperate forest and see the changing seasons, go to
> www.usborne.com/quicklinks

Many animals prepare for the winter by storing up food. Some, such as the dormouse, cope with the lack of food by going into a deep sleep known as hibernation. During hibernation, an animal's breathing and heartbeat slow down and it does not need to eat. There are also animals that avoid the cold weather altogether by moving, or migrating, to warmer places.

A dormouse hibernating in its nest during the winter months

POLAR REGIONS

The Arctic, the area around the North Pole, and the Antarctic, the area around the South Pole, are known as the polar regions. The temperatures there are usually below freezing and huge expanses of land and sea are covered in ice and snow.

This map shows the Arctic from above. The imaginary line around it is called the Arctic Circle.

Arctic

The Arctic is mainly made up of the Arctic Ocean, but its edges are bordered by several countries, including Greenland, Canada and Alaska. The land here, called the tundra, is just warm enough for animals and plants to survive.

In the summer, the ice on the tundra melts and the surface of the ground thaws. The ground often becomes boggy, because deeper down it is still frozen and the water cannot seep through. This frozen layer is called permafrost.

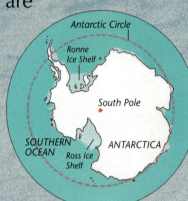

This map shows the Antarctic from above. The imaginary line around it is called the Antarctic Circle.

Antarctic

In the middle of the Southern Ocean is a land mass, or continent, known as Antarctica, which is covered in a thick layer of ice. Temperatures are so low that when snow falls it doesn't melt, but builds up with each snowfall. The weight of the snow on top presses down on the lower layers to form ice.

No land mammals live permanently in Antarctica because it is so cold, but some animals, such as seals, go there to breed. A number of sea birds, including penguins, live there permanently.

The emperor penguin is one of seven different species of penguins that live in the Antarctic.

Keeping warm

Some polar animals have adapted to living in the sea, as icy winds make it difficult to survive on land. For example, penguins cannot fly and seals move awkwardly on land, but both are good swimmers. Other animals have adapted to cope with the cold in different ways. Polar bears have a thick layer of fat under their skin which keeps them warm. Musk oxen have thick, shaggy coats. Many polar animals have small ears, which help to reduce heat loss.

These penguins are huddling together for warmth. They take turns standing on the outside.

The Arctic fox's white winter coat means that it doesn't stand out against the snowy background.

Blending in

A number of animals in the Arctic have different winter and summer coats. As the snow falls in the winter, their coats change and become white. This enables them to camouflage themselves, or blend in with their backgrounds. During the summer a brown coat helps them to blend in more easily with the grass. Their ability to change with their environment helps these animals to hide from predators or to sneak up on their prey without being seen.

Internet links

To watch video clips of Arctic and Antarctic animals and find out how they are adapted to polar life, and see animations about how icy landscapes are formed, go to
www.usborne.com/quicklinks

In summer, the Arctic fox's brown coat enables it to blend in with rocks and plants.

Arctic shelters

Some animals that live in the Arctic build burrows or dens in the snow to protect themselves from the cold winds. For example, polar bears build dens, with many chambers in the snow, for their cubs to take shelter.

MOUNTAINS

About 5% of the world's land surface is covered by high mountains and mountain ranges. Mountain areas have more than one type of climate because, as you go up a mountain, there are fewer particles in the air and the temperature falls.

The Great Basin Desert in Nevada, USA, lies on the sheltered side, or rain shadow, of the Sierra Nevada mountains.

Mountain ranges

Most mountains are formed when the plates that make up the Earth's crust push together, forcing the land into fold mountains*. This is why mountains often occur in long lines, or ranges.

When air flows from the sea onto a mountain range, it is forced to rise. Clouds form as a result of condensation and rain or snow then falls on the mountainside. The sheltered land on the other side of the mountain, called the rain shadow, gets very little rain, and may become a desert.

Mountain peaks in the Andes, on the border between Chile and Argentina

Mountain levels

The higher up a mountain you go, the colder it gets. This is because the air higher up is thinner, so it can store less heat. There are different types of weather, vegetation and animal life at different heights up the mountain. Few species live on the windy peaks, but mountain goats and sheep graze on the grassy, rocky slopes below. Farther down, below a line called the treeline, it is warm enough for trees to grow. Animals such as cougars and hares live in mountain forests.

Internet links
To watch video clips about mountain wildlife and explore some of the world's highest mountains, go to www.usborne.com/quicklinks

The Alpine forget-me-not flower is adapted to mountain climates. It has shorter, thicker stems and deeper roots than the common forget-me-not.

This shepherd from the Basque region of France is holding two baby goats. Goats are suited to the mountain climate.

Mountain dwellers

Both animals and people living in high mountain areas have bigger lungs to help them breathe more easily in the thin air. Animals need thick fur and people need thick coats to keep them warm. Mountain people may be cut off from other cultures. For example, the Basque people, who have lived in the Pyrenees mountains between France and Spain for thousands of years, have a very unusual language which is unlike any other on Earth. This is because, for centuries, they rarely mixed with other peoples.

*Fold mountains, 19

CHANGING CLIMATES

Ever since the Earth was formed, its climate has been changing. Volcanic eruptions, collisions with asteroids* and the path of the Solar System through space may all have caused climate changes that affected the atmosphere, the landscape and living things.

The red outline on this map shows the areas of the Earth that were covered in ice during the last Ice Age. The white areas are those places that are still covered in ice today.

Long ago, widespread volcanic activity could have caused fires which damaged habitats, wiping out various species.

Ice ages

Throughout its history, the Earth has gone through several ice ages, when the climate was colder than it is now, and glaciers* and ice sheets spread across much of the globe. Sea levels were lower as well, because so much of the water was frozen into ice on land.

Ice ages have several causes. As the galaxy spins, the Earth may enter the magnetic fields which shield it from the Sun's heat. Earth may also sometimes change its orbit, move away from the Sun and get cooler. There may be another ice age in the future.

Internet links

For links to websites where you can explore climate timelines, find out what fossils can tell us about the past and learn about mass extinctions, such as the disappearance of the dinosaurs, go to www.usborne.com/quicklinks

Explosions

Long-term climate patterns can be affected by sudden events, such as huge volcanic eruptions, or asteroids* hitting the Earth. Events like this in the past could have filled Earth's atmosphere with smoke and dust which blocked out the sunlight, making the climate cold and dark and killing plants and animals.

*Asteroids, 140; glaciers, 130

Geological evidence

We can tell the Earth's climate has changed by looking at rocks and fossils. Many rocks form gradually in layers. These layers provide a record of what happened, called the fossil record. In warmer periods of the Earth's history, more plants and animals were alive and more fossils were preserved. Layers with fewer fossils show colder periods, when there were fewer living things.

Landscapes also hold clues about the past. For example, a U-shaped valley shows where a glacier gouged out a huge channel during an ice age.

Fossils found in stone, such as this well-preserved bird fossil, can reveal which types of animals lived in which places long ago.

As well as blocking out vital sunlight with smoke and ash, volcanic eruptions can destroy plant life by smothering the land with lava, hot molten rock that burns everything in its path.

Moving continents

As the plates* that make up the Earth's crust have slowly changed position, the climate of each continent has altered. For example, what is now West Africa was once at the South Pole. As it got nearer the Equator, its climate warmed up as it received more sunlight. Climates are also affected by ocean currents*. As the continents separated from each other, currents could flow between them, bringing cold or warm water from other parts of the Earth.

*Ocean currents, 51; plates, 18

Frost on a window

WEATHER

WHAT IS WEATHER?

Weather is the way the Earth's atmosphere* behaves, whether it is hot or cold, windy or still, raining, snowing or hailing. Climate* means the overall temperature and patterns of weather in a particular place.

The importance of weather

Weather affects everyone's life. Anything from crops to summer vacations can be ruined if the weather behaves unexpectedly. Weather is also a factor in many of the world's worst disasters, such as floods, droughts and famines.

For thousands of years, people have worshipped weather gods and used rituals to try to affect the weather. But, even with modern technology, it is almost impossible to control.

Internet links

For links to websites where you can watch video clips about different types of weather, find out more about climate, and discover record-breaking weather facts, go to
www.usborne.com/quicklinks

This Japanese dancer wears a special costume as part of a traditional dance which is meant to make the rain fall.

*Atmosphere, 48; climate, 56; cumulus clouds, 81; evaporation, 80

What weather is

Weather is made up of three main ingredients: temperature, the movement of the air, and the amount of water in the air.

Hot weather is caused by the Sun heating up the land and the atmosphere*. If the Sun is hidden by clouds, or if a cold wind is blowing, the temperature is cooler.

Wind is also caused by the Sun. As air gets hotter, it expands, gets less dense, and rises. A mass of colder, heavier air rushes in to replace it, making wind.

Finally, the Sun's heat makes water from plants, soil, rivers and seas evaporate* into the air. High up, this condenses into water droplets which form clouds, and may then fall as rain, snow or hail.

These factors are always changing and affecting each other. They combine to make complicated patterns, known as weather systems.

Traditional signs

Cumulus clouds usually appear when the weather is warm and sunny.

Today, scientists can predict the weather using satellites and computers. But before these were invented, people predicted the weather by observing signs, such as the way the clouds look, and the way animals behave. For example, cumulus clouds* usually mean sunny weather, and bees usually go home to their hives before a storm.

The way bees behave could help us predict the weather.

Weather facts

• The heaviest hailstones, weighing up to 1kg (2lb 2oz), fell in Gopalganj, Bangladesh, in 1986.

• The wettest place in the world is Mawsynram, India. It gets nearly 12m (40ft) of rain a year.

• The biggest recorded snowflakes were 38cm (15in) across and fell on Montana, USA, in 1887.

• The driest place in the world is the Atacama Desert, Chile. In some spots, there has been no rain for 500 years.

Umbrellas have been used for hundreds of years to protect people from the weather. These paper umbrellas, called parasols, help to protect people from the Sun.

WATER AND CLOUDS

The amount of water on Earth doesn't change, but water changes its state as it moves in a cycle. It exists as a liquid (water) in seas, rivers and cloud droplets, it freezes into a solid (ice) as snow and hail, and it exists as an invisible gas in the air.

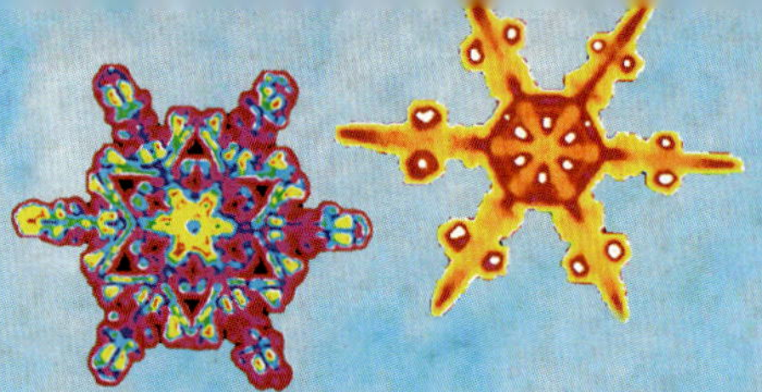

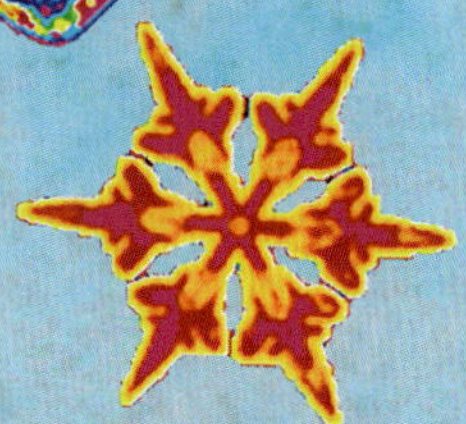

Snowflakes form when water droplets freeze into ice crystals. These snowflakes have been tinted so you can see their six-sided shapes more clearly.

The water cycle

When water is heated up, it changes from a liquid into an invisible gas. This process is called evaporation.

The Sun's heat causes water to evaporate from rivers, lakes and seas. Plants suck up water from the ground and it escapes from their leaves as a gas. Similarly, people and animals breathe out water as a gas.

As the gas molecules rise, they get cooler. This makes the water condense, or turn into liquid again, to form tiny droplets which can be seen as clouds. As the cloud droplets move around they collide with each other and grow bigger. When they are heavy enough, they fall as rain, and the water flows back into rivers, lakes and seas. This process is known as the water cycle.

When cloud droplets become heavy, they fall as rain, snow or hail.

Water flows down to the sea in streams and rivers.

As the water that has evaporated rises, it cools down to form clouds.

Plants and animals take in water that has fallen as rain.

Water evaporates from rivers and seas in the heat of the Sun.

This diagram shows how the water cycle works.

Clouds

The way clouds look depends on how much the air is moving up and down and how much water is in them. When clouds form in calm air, they spread out in sheets. On hot days, they puff up into heaps, following the rising air. Clouds full of big droplets look darker.

These tall, piled-up cumulonimbus clouds were photographed over the Gulf of Mexico. A cumulonimbus cloud is freezing at the top, but warmer at the bottom.

Cumulus clouds look like white, puffy heaps. They often form high in the sky in warm sunny weather.

Stratus clouds form low, flat layers and often block out the sunshine.

Cirrus clouds are high and wispy. (The word cirrus means "like wispy hair" in Latin.)

Precipitation

Water that falls onto the Earth's surface is called precipitation. Rain is the most common kind. There are many types of rain, from light drizzle to monsoon rains*. In freezing weather, precipitation sometimes takes the form of snow or hail instead of raindrops.

This diagram shows how hailstones are formed.

Hail begins as ice crystals in giant cumulonimbus clouds.

Air currents push the crystals up and around inside the cloud.

As they move, the crystals bump into water droplets, which freeze around them in layers, like the layers of an onion.

The layers of ice build up until they form heavy hailstones, which fall to Earth.

Internet links
To watch video clips about different types of clouds, go to www.usborne.com/quicklinks

*Monsoons, 62

THUNDERSTORMS

Sometimes in warm weather, huge storm clouds form very quickly. These clouds are full of water and fast-moving air currents. They can build up a store of electricity powerful enough to make lightning and thunder.

Internet links
To watch videos about thunderstorms and how lightning forms, and browse amazing photos of lightning, go to www.usborne.com/quicklinks

Electric clouds

In hot, damp weather, the evaporated water in the air rises very fast. When it hits the colder air above, tall, piled-up clouds called cumulonimbus clouds form.

Inside the cloud, water droplets and ice crystals rub together in the swirling air. This rubbing causes the crystals and droplets to build up a strong electric charge. Some have a negative charge (–) and some have a positive charge (+). Negative charges collect at the bottom of the cloud, making a huge energy difference between the cloud and the ground, which has a positive charge.

The difference builds up so much that it has to be equalized. A giant spark jumps between the bottom of the cloud and the ground, allowing the different charges to even out. The spark appears as a flash of lightning.

The satellite photograph on the left shows piled-up cumulonimbus storm clouds viewed from above.

Lightning zigzags through the air as it finds the easiest path from the cloud to the ground.

Ball lightning is a very rare kind of lightning which appears as a small, floating ball of bright light. It can travel through walls and has been seen inside buildings and aircraft.

Lightning

When lightning strikes, it travels first downward, then upward. The first stroke, called the leader stroke, is invisible. It jumps from the cloud to the ground. This creates a path for the main stroke, which sparks from the ground back up to the cloud.

The main stroke contains so much energy that it heats up the air around it. The heat makes the air expand quickly, causing an explosion. This is the loud noise of thunder.

Struck by lightning

Lightning always travels the shortest distance it can between a cloud and the ground. So it usually strikes high places, tall buildings or prominent objects such as trees or people.

Lightning quickly heats up whatever it strikes. When a tree is struck, the water in the tree boils instantly and turns into steam, which makes the trunk explode. But although lightning is dangerous, being struck is very rare. You can stay safe by avoiding trees and open spaces during storms.

WINDSTORMS

Because of the way the world spins, wind doesn't flow in straight lines, but swirls into spirals. Sometimes, wind spirals grow into terrifying storms, such as hurricanes and tornadoes, which contain the fastest wind speeds on Earth.

A satellite picture of Hurricane Katrina

Coriolis effect

Winds are caused by high-pressure air rushing toward low-pressure areas, called cyclones. But instead of moving straight into the cyclone, the air circles around it in a spiral. This is called the Coriolis effect, and it happens because the spinning of the Earth always pushes winds to one side.

Hurricanes

Hurricanes are very powerful windstorms that can be hundreds of miles wide and last up to ten days. They only form in warm, wet conditions, usually over the sea in tropical areas near the Equator. No one knows exactly what makes a hurricane start.

The warm, wet air has a very low pressure, so cooler winds spiral toward it.

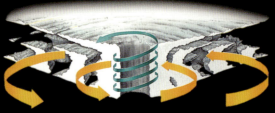

The damp air rises higher and condenses into thick clouds. They are blown into a spiral by the wind.

After hurricanes form, they sometimes hit land and cause massive damage. Winds of up to 240kph (150mph) destroy buildings and rip trees out of the ground. But hurricanes die down soon after they hit land, as there is not enough moisture to keep them going.

Tornadoes

Tornadoes are much smaller than hurricanes, but they can be even more dangerous. Tornadoes form during violent thunderstorms, when a hot, fast-moving upward air current meets a cold, downward air current. Because of the Coriolis effect, the hot and cold currents spiral around each other into a tight funnel of clouds.

The wind inside a tornado's funnel can be as fast as 480kph (300mph), the fastest wind speeds measured on Earth. Where the funnel touches the ground, it can be up to 500m (1,640ft) wide. It roars across the land, dragging people, animals and even cars into the air. Most tornadoes only last a few minutes.

Internet links

For links to websites where you can watch video clips of hurricanes and tornadoes and find out more about Tornado Alley in the USA, go to www.usborne.com/quicklinks

A tornado looks like a huge black or grey trunk, twisting from the thunderclouds down to the ground.

Tornado Alley

Some places have frequent thunderstorms and lots of tornadoes. Part of the USA, between Texas and Illinois, has so many that it is known as Tornado Alley. The worst tornado ever recorded there hit Ellington, Missouri, on March 18, 1925. It lasted 3½ hours, destroyed four towns and killed 695 people across three states.

Waterspouts

When a tornado moves over the sea a narrow column of swirling water droplets reaches into the clouds above. These tornadoes are called waterspouts (though not much water is actually sucked up from the sea). Sailors used to think they were sea monsters.

This 19th-century engraving shows monstrous waterspouts.

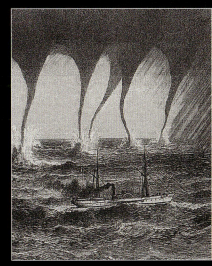

FLOODS AND DROUGHTS

Plants, animals and people need water to survive, and they rely on the weather to bring it to them. If there is too little rain, rivers dry up and crops fail. On the other hand, too much rain causes floods, which can damage crops and buildings and wash away precious soil.

Wet and dry

Some parts of the world always have more rain than others, and many places have wet and dry seasons. Rainy and dry periods like these are not usually a problem if they are regular, but too much or too little rain can be dangerous when unexpected weather changes take people by surprise.

This picture shows terrible flooding in Vietnam. People are forced to use boats to get around.

Too much rain

Normally, rainfall soaks into the ground or flows away in streams and rivers. Floods happen when there is suddenly too much water for the ground to hold, and streams, rivers and drains overflow. The extra water can come from rain, brought by heavy storms, from ice and snow on mountains melting and flowing into streams and rivers, or even from the sea spilling onto the land.

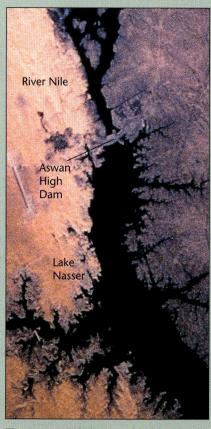

The Aswan High Dam enables people to control the flooding of the River Nile. When the river floods, it waters the land, making it fertile (good for growing crops) without causing destruction.

Dirt and disease

Floods are very dangerous. As well as drowning people and animals and destroying homes and crops, floods can actually cause water shortages. They cover the land with dirty water, contaminating clean water supplies and helping diseases to spread.

Lack of rain can make soil harden, crack into lumps, and eventually crumble into dry dust.

This pump is an important source of clean water, but the dirty floodwater surrounding it could contaminate the water supply.

Not enough rain

A drought happens when there is less than the expected amount of rain. Droughts are often hard to predict, but they usually happen when winds change direction and no rain clouds are blown over the land. Droughts can happen in almost all climates. A bad drought may last several years and make the land completely infertile. The effects of drought can be much worse if the land has not been used carefully.

Internet links

For links to websites where you can watch video clips about the effects of floods and droughts in different parts of the world, go to www.usborne.com/quicklinks

FREEZING AND FRYING

The temperature on Earth can range from a bone-numbing -88°C (-127°F), measured at Vostok in Antarctica, to an unbearably hot 56.7°C (134°F), recorded in Death Valley, California, USA. Extreme hot and cold weather can be deadly, and often has strange effects on people and places.

This woman is carrying frozen milk home. It is so cold in Siberia, where she lives, that there's no danger of the milk melting.

World of ice

Ice storms are caused by rain falling onto very cold surfaces. They happen when a mass of warm air passes through a cold area in winter, bringing rain that falls in the form of liquid raindrops, instead of snow or hail. But when the drops of water hit cold surfaces, they immediately freeze into a coating of solid ice. Ice storms are beautiful, but lethal. If enough rain falls, outdoor surfaces can get covered in a layer of ice up to 15cm (6in) thick. It makes roads hazardous to drive on and builds up on rooftops until they cave in.

The ice also weighs down power lines until they snap. People can freeze to death in their homes.

Blizzards

Blizzards are a combination of heavy snow, strong winds and cold temperatures. They are especially dangerous because blizzard victims are blinded by the swirling snow, and they can be caught in the freezing cold.

This branch was caught in an ice storm that hit Kingston, Canada, in 1998.

Internet links

For links to websites where you can visit the hottest and coldest places on Earth and discover how people cope with living in extreme climates, go to www.usborne.com/quicklinks

Heatwaves

A heatwave is a period of extra-hot weather. Heatwaves are caused by a combination of factors. Usually, a lack of wind and cloud allows the Sun to heat up the land and the atmosphere much more than normal. The hotter the air is, the more moisture it can hold as a gas. This makes the air very humid, which makes it feel "sticky".

In some hot places, people have siestas – they sleep during the hottest part of the day to avoid the Sun.

This Egyptian boy's white clothes reflect the Sun's rays and help to keep him cool in hot weather.

Heatstroke

Heatstroke is usually caused by staying out in the sun too long. Normally, if you get too hot, your body sweats. The sweat evaporating from your skin helps you cool down. But heatstroke stops your body from sweating so that you get much too hot, and may go into a coma.

Heatstroke can happen quickly, especially inside a car, where the windows act like a greenhouse and stop heat from escaping. This is why animals and babies should never be left inside cars on hot days.

Sun and skin

Although the Sun provides warmth and energy, direct sunlight can be bad for you. It can cause wrinkles, sunburn and even skin cancer.

This poster advises Australians to slip on T-shirts, slop on sunscreen and slap on hats.

Hot and bothered

Hot weather can affect how we behave. For example, statistics show that in New York, USA, the murder rate rises as the temperature goes up, and most big riots start on hot, humid nights. No one is sure why heat makes people angry.

This riot took place in the hot city of Los Angeles, in western USA, in 1992.

STRANGE WEATHER

Unusual, extreme weather, often called freak weather, can take people by surprise. Sometimes it can be so odd it doesn't seem like weather at all. Strange lights in the sky, clouds that look like UFOs, and even showers of frogs, are all natural weather phenomena.

Weather beliefs

When strange weather strikes, people often think they're seeing something magical or supernatural. Weather may lie behind many traditional beliefs in fairies and ghosts, and also behind sightings of UFOs. One type of cloud, called a lenticular cloud, looks exactly like a flying saucer.

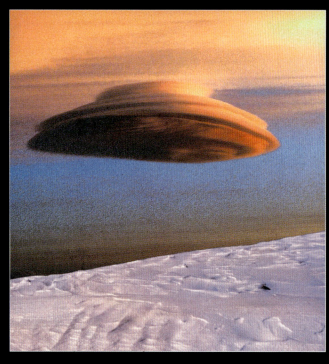

Lenticular clouds are shaped by waves of wind blowing around mountaintops. This one was seen at Mauna Kea, Hawaii, USA.

Strange lights

The aurora borealis and aurora australis light up the sky around the poles with blue, red, green and white patterns. They are caused by streams of electrical particles which come from the Sun. When they interact with the gases in the Earth's atmosphere, they release energy which lights up the sky.

A solar flare is a storm on the Sun that sends electrical particles out into space, causing auroras on Earth.

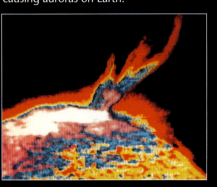

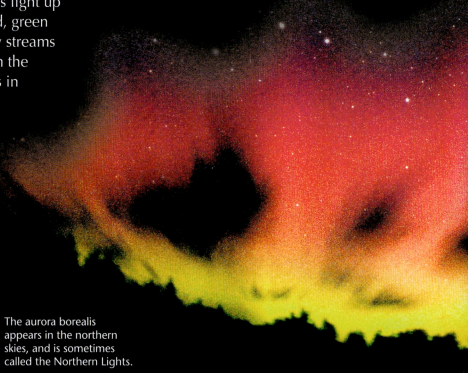

The aurora borealis appears in the northern skies, and is sometimes called the Northern Lights.

Raining frogs

"Rain" consisting of animals, fish or other objects has been reported many times through the centuries. The Roman historian Pliny reported a shower of frogs almost 2,000 years ago and in the fourth century, fish fell on a town in Greece for three days. During a storm in England in 1939, so many frogs fell that witnesses were afraid to walk around in case they squashed them.

Showers like this, also known as "skyfalls", are probably caused by tornadoes* sucking up animals from ponds and rivers. Frogs are most often reported, but there have also been showers of snails, maggots, worms, pebbles and even sheep.

The common frog, a species seen falling from the sky.

This magazine from May 1958 shows a skyfall of frogs which had recently been reported.

Internet links
To watch video clips of auroras and find out about weather folklore and legends, go to www.usborne.com/quicklinks

Freak waves

Freak waves are one of the most dangerous types of unusual weather, though not all big waves are freak waves. Freak waves can appear from nowhere, even in calm conditions. Scientists think big waves like this may form when several smaller waves merge together. These waves are especially dangerous because people are not prepared for them.

*Tornadoes, 85

WEATHER FORECASTING

Weather often seems random but, by careful observation, meteorologists (weather scientists) can learn how weather behaves and how to predict it. Radar and satellites* help them to track clouds and watch weather patterns from space.

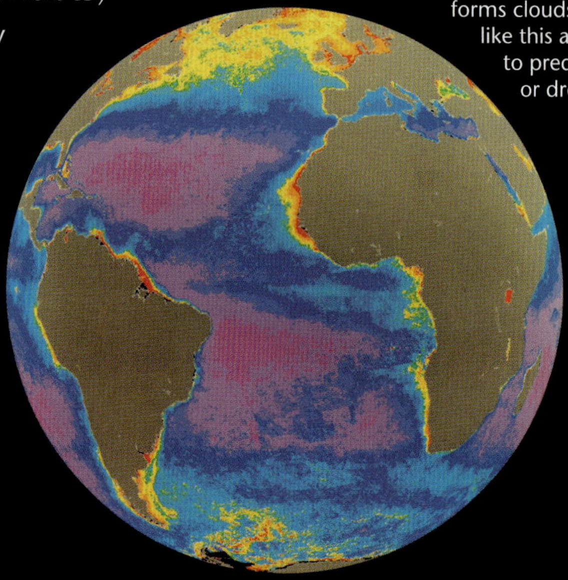

Measuring weather

Meteorologists measure different aspects of the weather, such as temperature, atmospheric pressure* and the amount of rainfall, at weather stations around the world. Weather balloons and weather planes carry instruments into the sky, where they can track the movements of clouds and high-altitude winds.

This satellite image shows the temperature of the sea. Water evaporates from warm areas (shown in pink) and forms clouds. Maps like this are used to predict rain or droughts.

Weather technology

Weather satellites have been used since about 1960 to record the Earth's weather from space. From their positions in orbit above the Earth, satellites can take photographs and measure the temperature of the Earth's surface.

Geostationary satellites, like the weather satellite shown here, hover 36,000km (22,370 miles) above the Equator.

On the ground, radar equipment is used to detect cloud patterns. Radar waves are sent out, bounce off raindrops and are collected by giant radar dishes. Computers collect the signals and create maps which show where rain clouds are heading.

*Atmospheric pressure, 50; satellites, 11

Predicting weather

To forecast weather, readings from weather stations and satellites are stored in powerful computers. The data can then be examined to detect patterns and make predictions. At the moment, meteorologists can only predict weather a few days in advance. Weather can change so quickly that the forecasts are sometimes wrong.

Internet links
To watch video clips about how scientists predict weather using satellites and computers, go to **www.usborne.com/quicklinks**

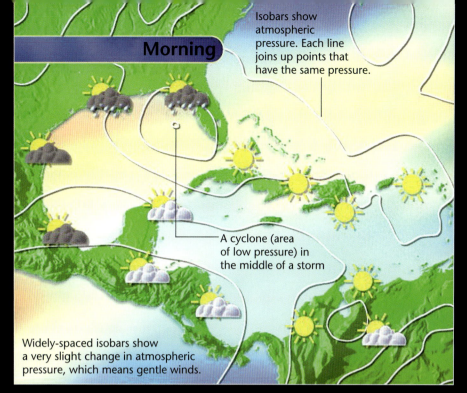

Morning

Isobars show atmospheric pressure. Each line joins up points that have the same pressure.

A cyclone (area of low pressure) in the middle of a storm

Widely-spaced isobars show a very slight change in atmospheric pressure, which means gentle winds.

Weather maps use lines called isobars to show differences in atmospheric pressure*, and symbols to indicate sunshine, rain and snow.

A digital photograph of Hurricane Gordon taken by a crewmember aboard the Space Shuttle Atlantis, in September 2006.

PLANTS AND ANIMALS

A red-eyed tree frog

PLANT LIFE ON EARTH

The Earth is the only planet known to support living things, or organisms. There are millions of different kinds of living things on Earth. They fall into two main groups: animals and plants. To survive, nearly all of them need light and heat from the Sun, food, water and air.

The Earth is the only planet so far discovered whose land looks green from space.

The green planet

Most plants are green because they contain a green substance called chlorophyll, which helps them to make their food. From space, the Earth's land looks mainly green, because of the billions of plants on its surface.

Plant food

Plants feed themselves by using sunlight to produce food chemicals. This process is called photosynthesis, which means "building with light". For this to happen, plants also need water and nutrients* from the soil, and carbon dioxide from the air. They then use all these things to make glucose, a kind of sugar, which they can feed on.

The Sun provides energy, in the form of light.

A plant's flowers contain parts that make seeds. These grow into new plants.

This part of the underside of a leaf has been magnified.

Leaves convert water and carbon dioxide into glucose and oxygen.

The stalk carries water and nutrients from roots to the leaves and flower.

Leaf stalk

Tiny holes called stomata let carbon dioxide in, and water and oxygen out.

Internet links

To find out more about the different types of plant life on Earth, how photosynthesis works and how plants survive in different habitats, go to www.usborne.com/quicklinks

*Nutrients, 112

Why we need plants

Plants are essential for life on Earth. Without them, the planet would look totally different, and there would be no people or animals. Animals – even meat-eaters – need plants, because plants form the basis of all food chains*. Plants also give out oxygen and water, which animals and people need; and their roots hold the soil together. Without them, much of the soil would wash away into the sea. We use plants to make medicines, food, fabrics and perfumes, and we get wood from trees.

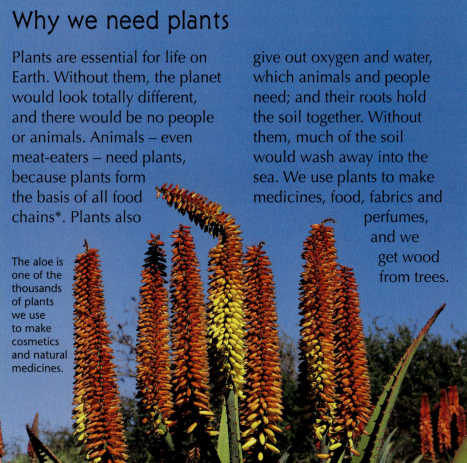

The aloe is one of the thousands of plants we use to make cosmetics and natural medicines.

Plant babies

Like all living things, plants reproduce (make new versions of themselves). Most do this by making seeds. The seeds usually form inside the flower. They may then be carried a long way by the wind before falling to the ground and beginning to grow.

A sunflower contains hundreds of seeds like these. Like the seeds of many plants, they are an important source of food for people and animals.

Types of plants

Different types of living things are called species. There are millions of species of plants, from tiny flowers to enormous trees called giant sequoias, which are the biggest living things on Earth. Different species are suited, or adapted, to living in different parts of the world. In deserts, for example, where water is scarce, cactuses grow thick stems for storing water.

A giant sequoia tree. These are found mainly in California, USA.

*Food chains, 100

ANIMAL LIFE ON EARTH

There are millions of types, or species, of animals living on Earth. They include insects, fish, birds, reptiles, amphibians and mammals, such as humans. Unlike plants, animals can move around to find food and water.

The bald eagle is a carnivore. It feeds mainly on fish, swooping down and snatching its prey from lakes and rivers.

How animals live

All animals have to eat in order to survive. Herbivores eat plants and carnivores eat animals. There are some animals, such as giant pandas, that eat both plants and animals. These are called omnivores. Most humans are also omnivores.

Honeyeaters are herbivores. They feed on nectar, a sweet juice found inside flowers.

Many animals have to watch out for predators, which are other animals that want to eat them. Their bodies have to be adapted for running fast or hiding. Some animals, such as zebras, are camouflaged, which means they are patterned so that they blend in with their background and are harder for predators to see. But some predators are also camouflaged, so they can creep up on their prey.

Tools for eating

Animals' bodies are adapted to suit the kind of food they eat. Herbivores usually have flat, broad teeth designed for munching plants, while most carnivores have sharp teeth to help them grab and grip their prey (the animals they eat) and tear raw flesh.

You can see the long, sharp teeth in this badger's skull. They are good for gripping and slicing through flesh.

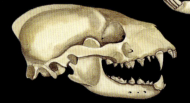

In this roe deer's skull, you can see the long front teeth which are suited to biting off pieces of plants and flat molar teeth which are good for chewing plants.

Natural selection

Why are animals and plants so well adapted to their way of life? One answer might be that they have gradually changed, or evolved, over a very long time to suit the places they live in and the food that is available to them. In the 19th century, a scientist named Charles Darwin (1809–1882) put forward a theory, which he called "natural selection", to explain how these changes might happen.

According to Darwin, individual animals and plants sometimes have qualities that help them to survive. For example, in a green forest, a green bug would probably survive longer than a brown bug, because its appearance would help it to avoid being seen and eaten.

The individuals that survive the longest are likely to have more babies, and will pass on their useful qualities to them. Over a very long time, each species will gradually develop all the most useful qualities for surviving in its own habitat.

Internet links
For links to sites where you can watch video clips about animal life on Earth and discover some of their special adaptations, go to www.usborne.com/quicklinks

Breathing

As well as eating food, animals need to breathe oxygen, a gas which is found in air and water. All animals take oxygen into their bodies, in a variety of different ways.

Gills

Fish have gills, which filter oxygen from the water as it flows through them.

Spiracles

Insects take in oxygen through tiny holes in their bodies, called spiracles.

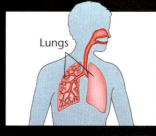
Lungs

Humans and many other animals have lungs, which extract oxygen from the air.

Useful animals

Animals are very useful to humans, providing meat, milk, eggs, wool, silk, leather and even medicines. Many animals are farmed carefully, but some species are in danger of dying out and becoming extinct, because humans have killed too many of them. You can find out about these endangered species on page 103.

Guanacos are hunted for their long, thick wool.

ECOSYSTEMS

A place where a plant or animal lives is called its habitat. For example, seas, rivers, mountains, forests and deserts are all habitats. Together, a habitat and the group, or community, of plants and animals that live in it form a whole system, called an ecosystem.

Meat-eaters survive by eating other animals found in their habitat. These cheetahs are chasing a Thomson's gazelle.

Snowy owls and lemmings are part of the ecosystem in the Arctic.

Food webs

In an ecosystem, many different food chains intertwine to make up a complicated system known as a food web. Each animal in the web may eat many different species and be hunted by several others. The diagram below shows part of a food web in a mountain forest in a northern country, such as Canada. Each blue arrow points from a species that is eaten to a species that eats it. (This is a simplified diagram. In fact, there would be many more species than this in one ecosystem, and the whole food web would be too complicated to fit on the page.)

Food chains

The animals and plants in an ecosystem depend on each other for food. One species eats another, and is in turn eaten by another. This is called a food chain. Plants form the first link in a food chain, because they make their own food from sunlight, using a process called photosynthesis*. Plant-eating animals (herbivores) eat plants, and meat-eating animals (carnivores) eat herbivores and other carnivores.

As in all ecosystems, plants form the basis of this food web.

*Photosynthesis, 96; soil, 112

Trophic levels

A food web has several layers, known as trophic levels. There are different kinds of plants or animals on each level.

The Sun provides light and energy for plants.

Tertiary consumers
Animals that eat other meat-eating animals

Secondary consumers
Animals that eat plant-eating animals

Primary consumers
Animals that eat plants

Producers
Plants that use the Sun's energy to manufacture food

Decomposers
Organisms that feed on dead plants and animals and break them down in the soil*

Internet links

To find links to websites where you can discover more about food chains, food webs and ecosystems, and watch video clips of herbivores and carnivores, go to www.usborne.com/quicklinks

Competition

Each type of plant or animal has a unique place in its ecosystem, known as a niche. If two different species try to compete for the same food, the stronger one survives, and the other dies out or has to move away. Different species in an ecosystem can survive side by side by eating slightly different types of food. For example, in African grasslands, elephants reach up to eat the higher branches of trees and bushes, gerenuks eat leaves lower down and warthogs nibble grasses on the ground.

The energy cycle

Plants and animals use food to make energy, which helps them grow, move, keep warm, make seeds and have babies. When plants or animals die, they are broken down by decomposers, such as fungi, and the energy goes back into the soil in the form of chemicals. These help plants to grow, and the cycle begins again.

Biomes

The Earth has several climate types, or biomes, such as rainforests and deserts. Each biome supports many ecosystems, but can also be seen as one big ecosystem. Together, all the biomes combine to form the biggest ecosystem of all, the Earth itself.

An elephant's long trunk allows it to reach to the tops of trees to collect food, while other animals eat the leaves lower down.

PEOPLE AND ECOSYSTEMS

Like every other plant and animal on Earth, you are part of an ecosystem. But there are now so many humans that we need more energy and make more waste than our ecosystem can deal with.

Using up energy

The first humans were suited to the ecosystems of the places they lived in. They ate the food that was available and used only as much energy as they needed to survive.

Now, though, we use up lots more energy than we really need to survive, because of all the things that modern humans do, such as running factories, getting around in cars and planes, and using electric lights and machines. We get most of our energy by burning fossil fuels*. This creates waste gases which can't be broken down quickly enough, so they build up around us as pollution.

Pollution

Pollution is any waste product that nature can't easily process and recycle. Things such as exhaust from cars, smoke from factories, and plastic packaging are all pollution.

Some pollution is just ugly, but some can be dangerous. For example, exhaust fumes that build up in the air can cause asthma, and chemicals that leak from farms into rivers can kill fish and upset the local food web*.

Smog is a kind of pollution caused when fossil fuels* are burned and give off waste gases.

Upsetting ecosystems

Each part of an ecosystem depends on all the other parts, making a natural balance. If one part is damaged or destroyed, it affects all the others.

If the plants in this food chain* were destroyed, the animals farther up the chain might starve.

*Food chains, 100; food webs, 100; fossil fuels, 24

Using up space

Our farms, cities, roads and airports all need space. We use space that used to be the habitats of plants and animals. Without its habitat, an ecosystem can't work, and animals and plants die. If this happens too often, some species become extinct, which means they die out completely.

Extinction is sometimes caused by natural disasters, such as volcanic eruptions, but often it is brought about by people. Pollution, hunting and introducing animals into new areas can all cause extinctions. For example, several species of flightless birds were wiped out when humans brought dogs and cats to Australia and New Zealand.

Wind turbines like these convert the energy of the wind into electricity. This causes less pollution than burning fuel.

The dodo, which lived on the island of Mauritius, died out in about 1680 after it was hunted to extinction by Dutch settlers.

Internet links

To find out more about the effects of pollution, endangered ecosystems and conservation projects to save rare wild animals and natural habitats, go to www.usborne.com/quicklinks

Conserving the Earth

Conservation means trying to reduce the damage done to the Earth and its species by pollution and other human activities. We can begin to conserve the Earth by using less energy, making less waste, and replacing as much as possible of the resources we use up. This is sometimes called sustainable living.

We cannot bring back plants and animals that are already extinct, but endangered species (those that are in danger of dying out) can be protected. Conservationists work to save natural habitats and protect rare wild animals from being hunted, so that they can build up their numbers.

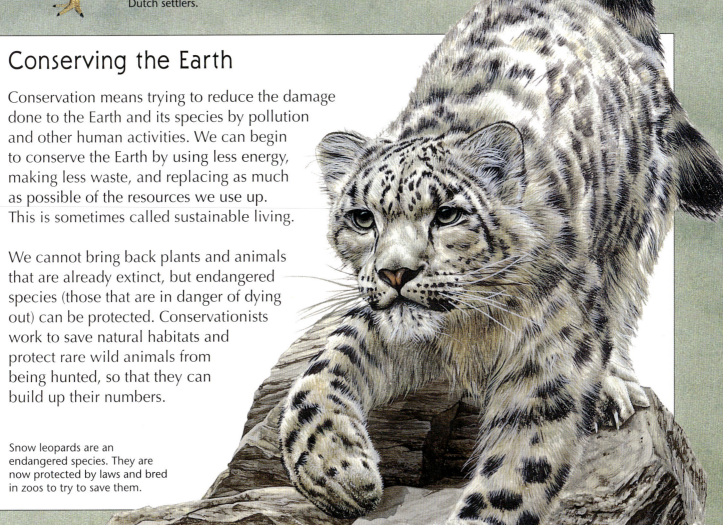

Snow leopards are an endangered species. They are now protected by laws and bred in zoos to try to save them.

POPULATION

Population is the number of people who live in a particular area. The population of the world has been rising for thousands of years, and is now going up faster than ever. In very crowded areas, it can sometimes be hard for people to get enough work, food or housing.

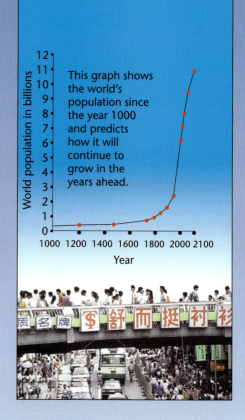

This graph shows the world's population since the year 1000 and predicts how it will continue to grow in the years ahead.

Counting people

With thousands of people being born and dying every day, it can be hard to measure population. Many countries hold a census, or population count, every ten years. Each household fills in a questionnaire, saying how many people live there. Experts use the results to estimate the population of a country at any one time, and to calculate the total population of the world.

Rising numbers

The world's population began to rise quickly in the 17th century, when there were about 500 million people on Earth. There are now over seven billion. Population is shooting up because the birth rate (the number of people being born in every 1,000) is higher than the death rate (the number of people dying in every 1,000). The death rate has dropped dramatically with advances in medicine and technology.

Finding a level

Population scientists, called demographers, predict that attempts to control population will eventually have an effect. They suggest the world's population total will reach 11 billion people by around 2100, then perhaps begin to level off.

Over and under

The world's population is not spread out evenly. Some areas are overpopulated, with not enough food, water or work for everyone. Other areas, such as the French countryside, are underpopulated, as young people leave the towns and villages for the big cities.

Population density

Population density is the number of people living in a given amount of space. It is measured in people per sq km or sq mile. For example, Mongolia (a big country with a small population) has a low population density of less than two people per sq km (five people per sq mile).

Internet links

To find out what the world's population was at the time of your birth and to explore how population growth affects the Earth, go to www.usborne.com/quicklinks

This map shows the average population density by country.

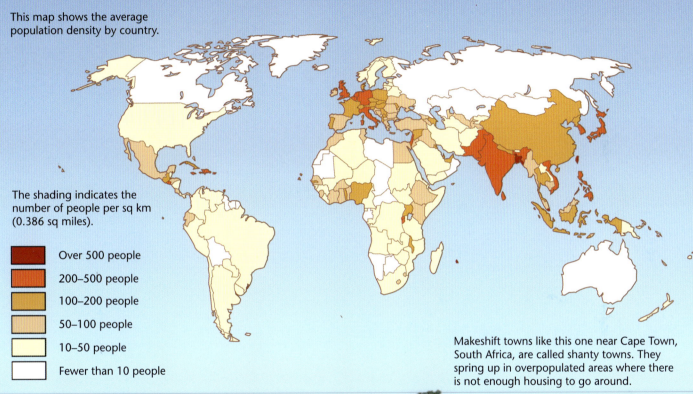

The shading indicates the number of people per sq km (0.386 sq miles).

- Over 500 people
- 200–500 people
- 100–200 people
- 50–100 people
- 10–50 people
- Fewer than 10 people

Makeshift towns like this one near Cape Town, South Africa, are called shanty towns. They spring up in overpopulated areas where there is not enough housing to go around.

FARMING

Farming means growing plants or raising animals to meet human needs. It is the biggest industry in the world and produces much of what you eat, wear and use.

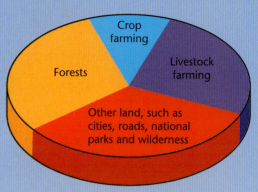

This pie chart shows how the world's land is used. Livestock farming uses more space than crop farming, but produces less food.

Types of farming

Growing plants is called crop farming or arable farming, and keeping animals is called livestock farming or pastoral farming. A mixture of both is called mixed farming. Farmers choose what to farm according to the type of land they have, the soil and the climate.

World industry

Around 45% of the world's workforce are farmers. Instead of just growing their own food, many farmers grow cash crops – crops grown specially to be sold and exported around the world. This is why, in some countries, you can buy different kinds of foods from all over the world in one supermarket.

Internet links

For links to websites where you can watch clips about different kinds of farms and find out about crops exported around the world, go to **www.usborne.com/quicklinks**

Yaks are adapted to surviving in high mountain areas. Farmers in the Himalayas keep them for milk and wool.

Wet soil and a warm climate are ideal for growing rice. In hilly areas, farmers build steps of land, or terraces, to hold the water and soil in place. This picture shows rice terraces in China.

Growing crops

Combine harvesters are used to gather all kinds of crops. It is much easier and quicker than harvesting fields of crop by hand.

Crop farming uses up around 11% of the world's land. It is the best way of producing as much food as possible from the soil, so poor countries usually grow a greater proportion of crops than rich countries do. Planting, protecting and harvesting (collecting) crops is hard work, but many farmers use machinery to do these tasks.

Animal care

Like crops, livestock has to be looked after carefully. The animals need food, water, shelter and protection from predators and diseases. Animal products also have to be "harvested", which means collecting the animals' milk, wool or eggs, or killing them for their meat.

Farm animals often have more than one use. We may use their wool or skins as well as meat. In many countries they also work, pulling carts or farm machinery.

Ostriches are farmed for meat, eggs and leather, and their feathers are used in fashion accessories.

FARMING METHODS

Farmers want to get as much as they can from their land. There are various ways of improving the yield, or amount of produce that comes from the land.

Helicopters like this are used by intensive farmers to spray fertilizers or pesticides onto their crops.

Choosing the best

An important part of farming is selective breeding, which involves choosing the best plants and animals and developing them to make more useful varieties. For instance, wheat started off as a type of grass called einkorn. When replanting, early farmers chose the einkorn with the biggest seeds because these would provide more food. Gradually, einkorn developed into modern wheat, which has lots of large seeds on each stalk.

Modern farmed wheat, developed from einkorn

A grass called einkorn

Internet links

For links to websites where you can find out more about different farming methods, including organic farming, go to **www.usborne.com/quicklinks**

Modern farm pigs, such as Landrace pigs (right), are descended from wild boar (below).

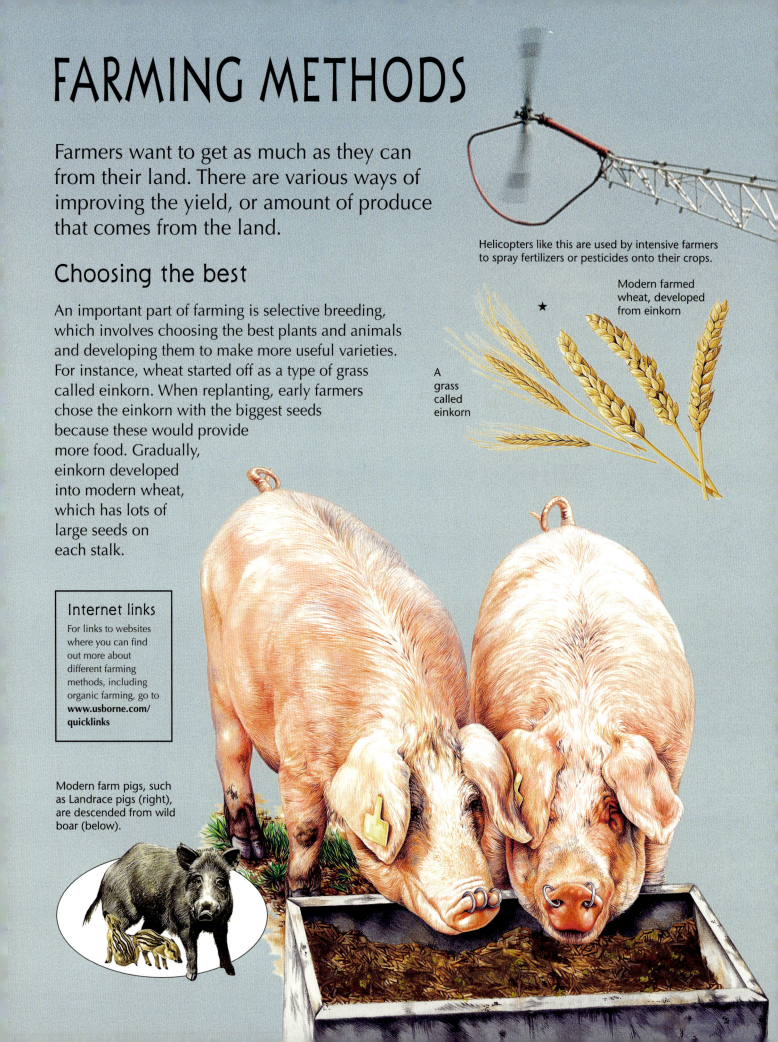

Some of the chemical spray used by farmers may be carried by the wind and affect other areas.

Chemical spray units attached to a helicopter

Intensive farming

Intensive farming means using chemicals and technology to get as much as possible out of the land. Intensively farmed animals, such as pigs or hens, are kept in small stalls or cages to save space. They are fed by automatic water and food dispensers and may be given drugs to make them grow faster. Intensive farming can increase yields, but the chemicals used can also cause pollution.

Some people think intensive farming is cruel, because the animals are kept in unnatural conditions. "Free range" animals live in more natural conditions and are allowed to move around, or range freely.

Intensively farmed battery hens live in small cages and are usually fed by machines. The eggs they lay roll into a tray and are carried away on a conveyor belt.

Organic farming

Organic farming means farming without using artificial chemicals or processes. Organic farmers use animal dung or compost instead of artificial fertilizer, and don't give animals drugs to make them grow faster. Organic food is expensive, because without drugs and artificial chemicals, diseases are harder to control and yields fall. However, there is a demand for organic products from people who are worried about their health, pollution and animal welfare.

Bug warfare

Insects and other bugs that eat farm crops can be a big problem. Intensive farmers (see right) often spray crops to kill insects, but organic farmers do not use chemical sprays. Instead, they sometimes try biological pest control. They change the ecosystem* in their fields by introducing another species to feed on the pest species.

These tiny aphids damage many crops. Instead of spraying, some farmers release ladybirds (ladybugs) to eat them.

*Ecosystems, 100

Pebbles on a beach in Oregon, USA

SHAPING THE LAND

SOIL

Soil covers over half of the Earth's land surface. It is vital to life on Earth, because it provides the food and conditions plants need to grow.

Internet links
For links to websites where you can find out about different types of soil, what's in it and why earthworms are important, go to www.usborne.com/quicklinks

As they burrow through the soil, earthworms drag dead leaves and other organic matter down to the lower levels, and break them down into humus.

What's in the soil?

Soil is made up of particles of rocks and minerals, dead plant and animal matter, tiny living organisms, gases and water. The particles of rocks and minerals range from big chunks of stone to tiny mineral particles which get dissolved by the water in the soil. Some minerals are taken in by plants and used as food. These are called nutrients. The dead plant and animal matter is gradually broken down into a substance called humus, by all the tiny creatures, bacteria and fungi in the soil.

Humus is what makes soil fertile (easy for plants to grow in). Living things are a vital part of the soil. If they weren't there to break down dead plants and animals, the remains of things that have died would keep piling up on the Earth's surface.

The water in the soil comes from rain, and gases come from the air and from plants and animals. Plants absorb water and gases through their roots.

This earwig and her babies are among the thousands of insects and other small animals that live in soil.

Soil layers

If you looked at a slice of soil under the ground, you would see that it has several different layers, called horizons.

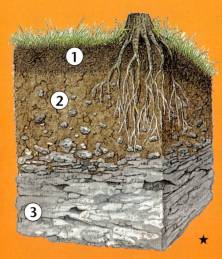

① The topsoil contains a lot of humus and is full of tiny living creatures.

② Subsoil is made up of humus, rocks and minerals. Cracks and holes, or pores, in the subsoil help water to drain away, preventing the soil from getting too wet.

③ The rock that lies underneath the soil is called bedrock. Chunks of it sometimes break off into the soil.

Types of soil

There are thousands and thousands of different types of soil. Some are more fertile than others, but different plants prefer different soils. Farmers can choose what to grow, depending on the type of soil they have on their land.

There are three main soil textures: sand, silt and clay. Sandy soil is rough and grainy. Silt has small particles, which are hard to see, while clay soil is made of fine particles, which bind together with water to form a thick, creamy mud. Clay is used to make pottery and china.

This picture shows parsnip roots reaching into the soil for water and minerals. Parsnips grow well in sandy and clay soils.

This hand contains sandy soil. Its grainy texture allows moisture to drain through it easily.

A handful of fertile soil contains up to six billion bacteria.

This hand contains loam soil. It is a very fertile soil containing a mixture of clay and sandy soils.

LOOKING AFTER SOIL

Why do we need to take care of soil? The answer is that pollution, farming and cutting down trees can all damage soil and upset its natural balance. If we want to keep using the soil to grow food, we have to protect it, and replace all the chemicals that farming takes away.

This farmer in Minnesota, USA, is loading up manure to spread over his land as a fertilizer.

The soil cycle

Where there is no farming, soil is part of a continuous cycle. Minerals are gradually dissolved into the soil. Dead plants and animals fall onto the ground, begin to rot, and are broken down into humus*. The minerals and the humus provide nutrients (food) for new plants, and the cycle starts again. This means that the nutrients that are taken out of the soil eventually get put back in.

But, when soil is used for farming, the crops are taken away to be sold, instead of rotting back into the ground. This causes the soil to become gradually less fertile* as it loses its nutrients.

Fertilizing

The best way to replace the nutrients in soil is to add a fertilizer. Fertilizers contain chemicals, such as nitrates, which plants need in order to grow. Manure (animal dung) is a natural fertilizer, but many farmers use specially made chemical fertilizers. Sometimes, if farmers use too much fertilizer, the chemicals can leak out of the soil into rivers, causing pollution.

Crop rotation

Crop rotation means changing the crop grown on a piece of land each year. It helps to keep the soil fertile, especially if the land is sometimes left to "lie fallow". This means the farmer doesn't harvest the crop, but lets it rot back into the soil. Plants such as legumes (peas and beans) and clover make good fallow crops because they put nitrates into the soil instead of taking them out.

Bright yellow oilseed rape is used to make cooking oil and as food for animals. Oilseed rape crops are often rotated with other crops on farms in Europe.

*Fertile, 112; humus, 112; terraces, 106

Soil erosion

In the natural environment, plants and trees hold soil together and stop it from being washed away by the rain or blown away by the wind. But when people chop down trees for firewood and farmers dig up the land to plant crops it leaves the bare soil exposed.

However, there are some ways to protect the soil. In some places, farmers can grow crops among the trees without cutting them down. If a main crop leaves bare patches of soil, a second crop called a cover crop can be planted in the gaps to stop it from eroding. In hilly areas, farmers build steps called terraces* into the hillside to hold soil in place.

This cover crop protects the soil between rows of rubber trees. It also lets farmers grow two crops on the same land.

Internet links

For links to websites where you can find out more about protecting soil and how pollution and cutting down trees harm soil, go to www.usborne.com/quicklinks

Lost forever

Ancient ruins show that there were once busy towns in places that are now desert, such as parts of Egypt and Saudi Arabia.

7,000-year-old pottery jars from an ancient civilization called Mesopotamia. The area where they were found is now desert.

The people who lived there may not have known how to look after soil and stop it from eroding. This may be why their civilizations died out.

With the trees cut down, the soil on this hillside could soon be washed away.

WEATHERING

The holes in this limestone on Kangaroo Island, Australia, were caused by acid in rainwater eating away at it.

The rocks that make up the Earth's surface are constantly being broken down by the weather and by the actions of plants and animals. This process is known as weathering.

Chemical weathering

Chemical weathering is usually caused by rainwater. The water absorbs gases from the air and the soil, making a weak acid. The acid eats away at certain types of rocks, creating cracks and holes which then let in more water and grow bigger.

Internet links

To find out more about how rocks are broken down by weather, plants and animals, and see examples of weathering, go to www.usborne.com/quicklinks

Physical weathering

Heat makes most substances get bigger, or expand. When rocks are warmed by the Sun, they expand, and when they cool down at night they shrink, or contract. The outer layer of the rock expands more, because it is directly exposed to the Sun's heat. Eventually it separates from the rock and peels off. This is called exfoliation.

A type of weathering called freeze-thaw action occurs when water seeps into cracks in rock and then freezes and expands.

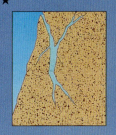 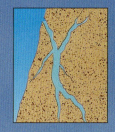 

The process of freeze-thaw action begins when rain seeps into a small crack in rock.

The water freezes, expands and widens the crack. When the ice thaws, more water can seep in.

As the temperature rises and falls, the crack gradually grows until the rock breaks apart.

Biological weathering

Weathering caused by plants or animals is called biological weathering. For example, lichens, which are small organisms that grow on rocks, give out acidic chemicals which eat away at the rock surface. Animals burrowing and roots growing in the ground can also contribute to rocks breaking down.

As well as being dissolved by acidic rainwater, the Kangaroo Island rock on the left is being eaten away by lichens – the red areas on its surface.

Shaping the landscape

Because some rocks are harder and more resistant to weathering than others, they wear away at different rates. Harder rocks get left behind as outcrops, which stick up out of the surrounding land, or as long ridges. Over many years, weathering can produce amazing rock shapes, jutting mountain peaks and deep limestone caves*.

This cave is still being shaped by chemical weathering, as acidic water eats away at cracks in the rock.

*Limestone caves, 129

EROSION

Erosion happens when wind, water, ice and gravity carry away particles of rock and soil that have been worn down by weathering*. Gradually, eroded material is carried downhill and into rivers, and most of it ends up being washed into the sea.

You can sometimes tell old mountains from younger ones by how worn and flattened they are.

K2 in the Himalayas is 8,612m (28,253ft) high. It is relatively young and still has pointed peaks.

Mount Baker in Washington, USA, is 3,285m (10,778ft) high. It has a flatter, worn shape, showing it was formed earlier in the Earth's history.

Wind and rain

Over hundreds of years, wind gradually blows away tiny particles from the surface of rocks. Many rocks contain different minerals, some harder than others. The wind wears them away at different rates, carving the rocks into wind sculptures.

Rain splashing onto rocks and soil washes away bigger particles and carries them into rivers. Farmers have to protect the soil* to prevent it all from eroding away in the rain.

These pinnacles in Arizona, USA, are striated, which means the wind has carved their surfaces into narrow grooves.

Moving mountains

On mountains, particles of rocks and soil are pulled downhill by gravity. Chunks of rock that break off near the top of a mountain fall down the slopes, knocking off other chunks as they go. Often a covering of loose stones, called scree, collects at the bottom of a slope.

Humans can add to this kind of erosion. Rock climbers sometimes dislodge scree and set off rockfalls, and walkers can slowly wear mountain paths away.

Wearing flat

As erosion carries particles of rocks and soil away from mountains and high ground toward the sea, the Earth's land masses become lower and smoother. However, new islands and mountains are sometimes formed by volcanoes* erupting and by the plates* that make up the Earth's crust grinding together. So as old land is worn away, new land rises up to replace it.

This photo shows the bare hillside left behind after a landslide in North Carolina, USA

Internet links

To explore landscapes that have been created by different types of erosion and find out more about landslides, go to www.usborne.com/quicklinks

Landslides

A landslide is a mass of soil and rock suddenly slipping down a steep slope. Many landslides are caused by rainwater soaking into the soil and making it heavier. Landslides are particularly likely if water soaks into a layer of shale (a type of slippery rock made from compressed clay).

Preventing erosion

A certain amount of erosion is normal, and we could never stop it completely. In some places, though, we can try to slow it down.

On mountains that are popular with walkers, stone or wooden paths help to protect the land from being worn away by feet. In hilly areas, trees help to keep the soil in place and prevent landslides, so people have learned not to cut down hillside trees.

A worker planting vegetation to prevent erosion near a roadside

*Plates, 18; soil erosion, 115; volcanoes, 28; weathering, 116

A group of Atlantic salmon swimming

RIVERS AND OCEANS

RIVERS

The water in rivers comes from rainfall, from snow and ice melting, and from water inside the Earth, called groundwater. Rivers carry this water downhill to lakes and oceans.

Hippopotamuses live in and around slow, muddy rivers in Africa. This one has an egret on its head.

A river's course

A river changes as it flows downhill along its path, or course. Many rivers begin in mountain areas, where rain and melting ice run into steep, clear streams. Mountain streams cut narrow, deep valleys and join together as they flow downhill. Smaller streams and rivers that flow into a bigger river are called tributaries.

Mountain streams, like this one in Connecticut, USA, form series of mini waterfalls as they tumble down over the steep, rocky slopes.

Away from the mountains, the water flows more smoothly in broader channels and larger valleys. As the land levels out, the river starts to form large bends, or meanders.

Finally, the river widens out into a broad estuary, or sometimes splits to form a delta*, before flowing into the sea (or sometimes into a large lake). The part of a river where it meets the sea is called the river mouth.

Internet links

For links to websites where you can discover facts and watch video clips about major rivers of the world and learn about the wildlife that relies on them, go to **www.usborne.com/quicklinks**

Stonefly larvae live in mountain streams. They cling to stones with their claws so they don't get swept away by the water.

Drainage

The area of land from which a river collects its water is called its drainage basin. When water drains into streams and rivers, it forms different patterns, depending on the shape of the land and the type of rock it is made of.

When there is only one type of rock, streams form a tree-like pattern like this. It is called a dendritic drainage pattern.

River records

The Manu River, a tributary of the Amazon, winding its way through the rainforests of Peru

The longest river in the world is the River Nile in Africa. It travels northward for 6,671km (4,145 miles) from its source in Burundi to its delta in Egypt, where it flows into the Mediterranean Sea. However, the world's biggest river, or the one that holds the most water, is the Amazon in South America. It is about 6,437km (4,000 miles) long, and flows across South America from west to east. Every single second, it pours about 94 million litres (20 million gallons) of water into the Atlantic Ocean. At its mouth, the Amazon is 240km (150 miles) wide.

A Nile crocodile stalks its prey by swimming silently along in the river, with most of its body underwater.

*Deltas, 124

RIVER EROSION

Rivers can carve through solid rock and move huge boulders hundreds of miles. Over many years, rivers have eroded deep gorges and huge waterfalls, and carried vast amounts of rock, sand, soil and mud to the sea.

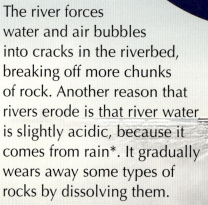

This satellite photo shows the Mahakam River, in Indonesia. You can see how a network of channels and islands, or a delta, is formed where the river runs into the sea.

How rivers erode

As a river flows, the water sweeps along any loose soil, sand or rocks in its way. As they roll, slide and bounce along, the rocks and pebbles chip away at the riverbed, making it deeper and wider. They also grind against each other, which wears them down and breaks them into smaller pieces.

The river forces water and air bubbles into cracks in the riverbed, breaking off more chunks of rock. Another reason that rivers erode is that river water is slightly acidic, because it comes from rain*. It gradually wears away some types of rocks by dissolving them.

Deposition

In its upper stages, a river is very turbulent and has lots of large boulders and pebbles on its bed. As it flows downstream the riverbed becomes smoother, so the water flows slightly faster. It starts to drop, or deposit, sand, silt and then mud. This is why the lower sections of a river have muddy beds. Near the sea, the deposited sediment may build up to form whole islands. The river splits up and forms a network of channels called a delta. The rest of the sediment flows into the sea.

These rocks have been smoothed and rounded by the action of the water in the river.

*Meander, 122; rainwater, 116

Changing course

Rivers flow faster around the outside of a meander* than on the inside. The outside edge is slowly eroded, while the river deposits debris on the inside edge. Eventually the two sides of the meander meet, and the river cuts through to form a new course.

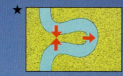
A river erodes the outside of a meander and deposits sediment on the inside, making a loop.

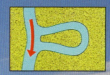
The loop grows longer and narrower until the river finally breaks through.

The river flows past the ends of the loop and they slowly become silted up.

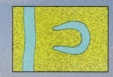
Eventually the loop gets cut off completely and forms a lake called an oxbow lake.

Internet links

For links to websites where you can find out about different river features, river erosion and how rivers change over time, go to **www.usborne.com/quicklinks**

This is the Horseshoe Falls, part of Niagara Falls, which is a huge waterfall on the border between Canada and the USA. The waterfall moves upstream by around 3m (11ft) per year.

Waterfalls

Waterfalls begin when a river flows from an area of hard rock onto soft rock. The river wears away the soft rock more quickly and creates a ledge. Water falling over the ledge erodes a hollow at the bottom called a plunge pool. The action of the water and pebbles churning in the plunge pool can undercut the hard rock, creating an overhanging ledge. Chunks of the overhanging rock break off and very gradually, over hundreds of years, the waterfall moves backward, cutting a deep valley called a gorge.

This diagram shows how a waterfall is formed.

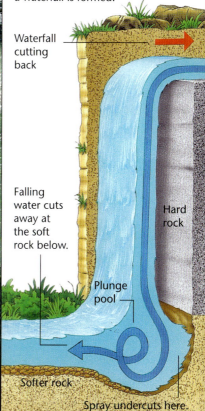

USING RIVERS

Rivers are central to the way human civilization has developed. They have been used for thousands of years for drinking and washing and as transport routes. Farming and industry depend on the water they provide and we can convert their flowing force into useful energy.

This engraving shows London, England, in 1631, with large ships plying their trade up and down the River Thames.

Amsterdam in the Netherlands is not on the sea, but is an important port, with over 80km (50 miles) of canals dividing it into over 80 islands.

River ports

A port is a city where ships can load and unload. When most international transport was by sea, many large ports, such as Montreal in Canada, Manaus in Brazil, and London in England, grew up near navigable rivers, that is rivers that can be used by ships. For example, most of the Amazon is navigable, because it is so wide and deep.

Canals

Canals are artificial waterways built to replace or extend rivers. Irrigation canals divert water from rivers onto fields. Navigational canals are built for boats or ships to travel on. For example, the Suez Canal joins the Mediterranean Sea to the Red Sea, so that ships can take a short cut between Europe and the Indian Ocean. The beds and banks of canals are usually built of brick or concrete, so they suffer less erosion* than natural rivers.

Internet links

For links to websites where you can investigate the many ways we use rivers as ports, canals, transportation routes and to generate energy, go to www.usborne.com/quicklinks

*River erosion, 124

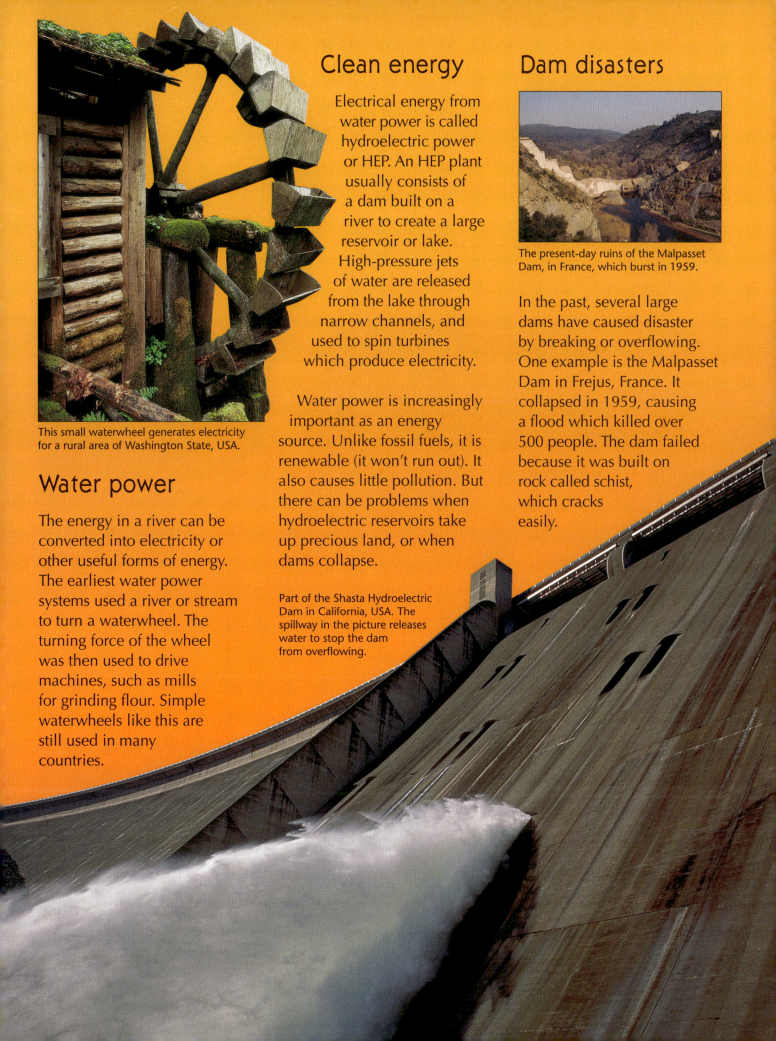

This small waterwheel generates electricity for a rural area of Washington State, USA.

Water power

The energy in a river can be converted into electricity or other useful forms of energy. The earliest water power systems used a river or stream to turn a waterwheel. The turning force of the wheel was then used to drive machines, such as mills for grinding flour. Simple waterwheels like this are still used in many countries.

Clean energy

Electrical energy from water power is called hydroelectric power or HEP. An HEP plant usually consists of a dam built on a river to create a large reservoir or lake. High-pressure jets of water are released from the lake through narrow channels, and used to spin turbines which produce electricity.

Water power is increasingly important as an energy source. Unlike fossil fuels, it is renewable (it won't run out). It also causes little pollution. But there can be problems when hydroelectric reservoirs take up precious land, or when dams collapse.

Part of the Shasta Hydroelectric Dam in California, USA. The spillway in the picture releases water to stop the dam from overflowing.

Dam disasters

The present-day ruins of the Malpasset Dam, in France, which burst in 1959.

In the past, several large dams have caused disaster by breaking or overflowing. One example is the Malpasset Dam in Frejus, France. It collapsed in 1959, causing a flood which killed over 500 people. The dam failed because it was built on rock called schist, which cracks easily.

WATER IN THE GROUND

Water doesn't just flow over the surface of the Earth; it flows under it too. As well as the rivers and lakes that we can see, there is a huge amount of water, called groundwater, stored underground in rocks and caves.

Bottling mineral water and spring water to sell as drinking water is a major industry in some areas.

Groundwater

Many types of rocks are permeable, which means that water can soak through them. Water that has soaked into the ground and then been soaked up, or absorbed, into a layer of permeable rock is known as groundwater. Underground, the upper layers of rock press down on the lower layers, compressing them so that they are less permeable. So the amount of groundwater decreases farther down. The top level of the water-soaked layer is known as the water table.

Aquifers are layers of rock that can hold water. Some stretch for thousands of miles under the ground. In some places they are an important source of fresh water.

Springs

A spring is a stream of fresh water springing out of the ground. Springs form where a layer of water-filled rock meets the surface of the Earth, especially on a hillside. The groundwater flows out of the rock and forms a small pool or stream.

Spring water is often clean and sparkling because it has been filtered through layers of rock. Sometimes the water dissolves minerals from the rocks. Some of these minerals are thought to be good for your health.

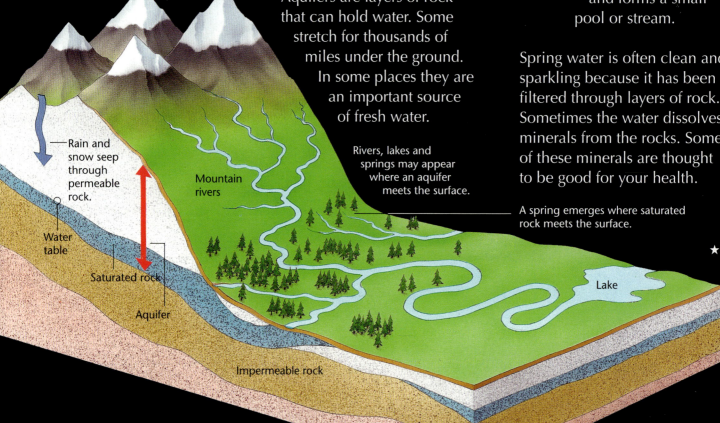

Rain and snow seep through permeable rock.
Water table
Saturated rock
Aquifer
Mountain rivers
Rivers, lakes and springs may appear where an aquifer meets the surface.
A spring emerges where saturated rock meets the surface.
Lake
Impermeable rock

Rivers under the ground

Water can also be found in underground rivers, waterfalls and even large lakes in caves and tunnels. These usually form in limestone. The water eats away at the rock through chemical weathering*.

> **Internet links**
> To find out more about groundwater including aquifers and springs, and rivers and lakes in caves and tunnels, go to www.usborne.com/quicklinks

Stalactites and stalagmites

In some caves, long columns of stone, called stalactites, hang from the ceiling, and columns called stalagmites rise up from the floor. They are formed when water full of dissolved minerals drips from the cave roof. With each drop, a tiny deposit of rock is left behind and over time this grows into a long column. As the drips hit the ground, they deposit more minerals, which build up into stalagmites.

These stalactites are constantly growing as more water drips off them, depositing a tiny amount of dissolved rock with each drip.

Inside this cave in Mexico, long stalactites have grown down from the ceiling, while water has gathered to form a still underground pool.

*Chemical weathering, 116

RIVERS OF ICE

> **Internet links**
> For links to websites with video clips and photo galleries of glaciers, fjords, continental ice sheets and icebergs, go to www.usborne.com/quicklinks

A glacier is a huge mass of ice that flows downhill, a little like a river. Glaciers flow much more slowly than rivers. But, because they are solid, they cut through the landscape more easily, gouging deep U-shaped valleys as they carry rocks and soil along with them.

This is a glacier in Glacier Bay National Park, Alaska, USA.

Ice force

Glaciers are very heavy and powerful. As a glacier flows along, the ice and rocks caught in it scrape soil and rock from the sides and floor of the valley, carving a deep channel. When the ice melts, it deposits thick layers of debris, called moraine, and boulders, known as erratics, on the valley floor.

How glaciers form

Glaciers are found in cold places, such as high mountains. At the top of a glacier, known as the accumulation zone, layers of snow collect and become packed down into hard, solid ice. As more snow falls on top, the mass of ice gets heavier and heavier, until it starts to move down the mountain.

As the ice gradually flows downhill, it gets warmer, because the air is warmer lower down. At the lower end, called the ablation zone, the glacier melts and the icy-cold water, known as meltwater, flows into streams and rivers.

Fresh snow falls here.

Accumulation zone

As a glacier moves over bumps and around corners, it may develop cracks called crevasses.

Boulders carried along by the glacier scratch grooves in the rock below.

The glacier melts here.

Ablation zone

Meltwater

This diagram shows the different parts of a glacier and the way it moves downhill.

Glacial clues

If the climate gets warmer, glaciers sometimes melt, leaving behind a glacial valley. You can recognize a glacial valley by its deep, rounded U-shape and by debris, such as boulders and moraine hills, or drumlins, left on the valley floor. Sometimes, valleys called hanging valleys, that once joined the glacier, are left high above the main valley. At the coast, some glacial valleys are filled with seawater. They form narrow inlets called fjords.

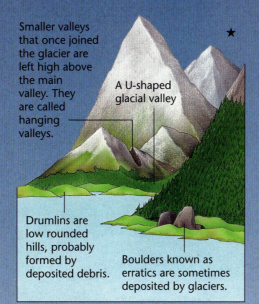

This diagram shows some of the features that will help you to recognize a glacial valley. A glacial valley filled with seawater, like this, is called a fjord.

Smaller valleys that once joined the glacier are left high above the main valley. They are called hanging valleys.

A U-shaped glacial valley

Drumlins are low rounded hills, probably formed by deposited debris.

Boulders known as erratics are sometimes deposited by glaciers.

Ice sheets

Not all glaciers are found on mountains. They also form in very cold places near the poles, such as Greenland and Antarctica. There, ice collects in huge sheets, called continental ice sheets. The ice flows outward at the edges as more snow falls and more ice forms in the middle. Parts of the glacier can be pushed right into the sea and break off, forming icebergs.

Icebergs float away into the ocean, gradually melting as they reach warmer areas.

THE EDGE OF THE SEA

The coast, where the land meets the sea, is constantly being broken down and built up by the action of waves. The ebb and flow of the tide means that the environment at the seashore is always changing. Specially adapted animals and plants make their homes there.

Internet links
To explore beach and coastline formations, see how waves erode land and form beaches, and find out more about tides, go to www.usborne.com/quicklinks

Waves

Waves are formed far out at sea by the wind. Although they travel through water, they do not move the water itself forward. They make water particles move in circles under the surface. When a wave reaches shallow water, these circles are interrupted at the bottom and the wave breaks.

Out at sea, wind blows the surface of the ocean into waves.

The waves make particles of water move in circular patterns under the surface.

On a shallow, flat beach, waves break before they reach the shore.

On a sloping coast, waves break at the shore and crash onto the beach.

On a very steep slope, waves do not break, but surge against the shore.

Coastal erosion

This archway in Dorset, England, is called Durdle Door. It was created over many years by the destructive action of waves. It started as a headland with caves on either side. The waves gradually eroded the caves until, eventually, they broke through, creating an arch.

Waves that crash onto the shore are known as destructive waves, because they gradually wear away, or erode, the coast. When they break onto beaches, they drag sand, pebbles and other debris out to sea. When they crash onto rocky cliffs, any debris they are carrying is flung against the rock, wearing it down. Waves force water and air into cracks in cliffs, carving out caves.

Destructive waves erode the coastline at different rates. Soft rock wears down quite fast, and is worn away into curved bays. Hard rock is left behind, forming cliffs and jutting pieces of land called headlands. Sometimes two caves form on either side of a headland, and the sea breaks through, leaving an arch. The arch may collapse, leaving a tower of rock called a stack.

*Tides, 149

Building beaches

While destructive waves wear away parts of the coast, other waves, called constructive waves, wash up debris onto the shore, forming beaches. When a wave breaks gently onto a flat coast, it slows down and loses energy. This makes it drop any debris it may be carrying, such as pebbles and grains of sand previously broken off into the sea from cliffs and rocky shores. Over time, this deposited material builds up into a beach.

Stones and pebbles in the sea are polished and rounded by the action of the waves.

Tides

Tides* are caused by the gravity, or pulling force, of the Moon. The Moon pulls the sea slightly towards it. So, as the Earth spins, the part nearest the Moon has a high tide. There are roughly two high tides each day.

Animals and plants that live on the seashore have to be able to survive in the water at high tide, and in the air at low tide. They also have to find ways to avoid being smashed to pieces or swept away by crashing waves.

Crabs, like this rock crab, can breathe in both water and air. They have hard shells to protect them from the sea, and can burrow into the sand to hide from predators.

Coastlines

Over many years, the action of the sea changes the shapes of countries, as it builds up the land in some places and wears it away in others. Buildings near the sea sometimes fall in or get washed away as the land is gradually eroded.

For example, the coast of Holderness in Lincolnshire, England, has worn away quickly. Over 50 coastal villages listed in a national survey of towns and villages called the Domesday Book in 1086 have since been washed into the sea.

SEAS AND OCEANS

More than two-thirds of the Earth's surface is covered with salt water. The Earth's five oceans and its seas are all connected, so sea water flows freely among them. The seas and oceans, and the creatures that live in them, still hold many mysteries for scientists to explore.

The ballan wrasse fish is found mainly near rocky shores in Europe.

Under the sea

Near the land, the seabed slopes gradually downhill, forming a wide shelf called the continental shelf. At the edge of the shelf, a cliff called the continental slope drops away to the deeper part of the ocean floor, which is called the abyssal plain.

A 3-D map of part of the floor of the Atlantic Ocean

Just like the land, the abyssal plain has valleys, hills, mountains and even volcanoes. It also has ridges* where new rock is pushed out from inside the Earth, and trenches* where the Earth's crust is swallowed up again.

Exploring the sea

By studying the seabed and the creatures that live there sea scientists, called oceanographers, can find out about how the Earth was formed and how life began. Oceanographers visit the seabed in mini-submarines called submersibles, or explore it from the surface using unmanned robots called remote operated vehicles (ROVs). They also map the seabed using sonar. This sends out sounds which are bounced back as echoes, showing how deep the seabed is.

This diver is retrieving a rock from a remote operated vehicle (ROV). The ROV has returned to shallow waters after collecting rock samples from the seabed.

*Ridges, 18; trenches, 18

Life in the oceans

Seas and oceans contain a huge variety of plant and animal life, from the surface all the way down to the deepest trenches.

The loggerhead turtle lives in warm, shallow seas and comes ashore to lay its eggs.

The main food source in the sea is phytoplankton, a type of microscopic plant. Billions of phytoplankton drift near the surface of the sea, making food from sunlight, water, gases and minerals.

Part of a coral reef in the Red Sea, which lies between Egypt and Saudi Arabia

Coral reefs

Coral reefs are amazing undersea structures made of the skeletons of tiny animals called coral polyps. When old polyps die, new ones grow on top of their bodies, and over many years a huge reef builds up.

Internet links

To watch video clips of life in the ocean and coral reefs, and discover how scientists explore under the sea, go to www.usborne.com/quicklinks

Ocean zones

The deeper down you go in the ocean, the darker and colder it is, and the fewer plants and animals are found.

Sunlit zone
Sea plants and many animals live here.

Down to 200m (650ft)

Twilight zone
Many fish, such as swordfish, survive here.

Down to 1,000m (3,300ft)

Sunless zone
Animals feed on dead food that falls from above.

Down to 4,000m (13,100ft)

Abyssal zone
The water is cold and dark. Few creatures live here.

Down to 5,000m (16,400ft)

USING SEAS AND OCEANS

For thousands of years, the sea has provided people with food. We also carry passengers and goods by sea and go on trips to the coast. But the oceans are often used as a place to dump waste, which causes pollution and may endanger wildlife.

Fishing

Most sea fish are still caught using nets. There are three main types of nets. Purse seine nets are drawn closed around schools of fish that swim near the surface. Otter trawl nets are dragged along the seabed to catch fish that live there, while drift or gill nets can be used near the surface or on the seabed. Fishing boats now find schools of fish by using sonar* and satellite* technology.

Above and top right: sea bass are the most common fish caught and eaten around the world. These were caught in Tokyo Bay, Japan.

Overfishing

Because of advances in fishing technology, fishing boats are now able to catch more fish than ever before, and the number of fish in the sea is falling rapidly. International laws have now been passed to restrict the areas where fishing boats can fish and the numbers and types of fish that can be caught.

A Japanese fishing boat at work in Tokyo Bay, Japan, drawing a large net behind it.

Internet links

For links to websites to help you understand the causes of ocean pollution, go to www.usborne.com/quicklinks

*Satellites, 11; sonar, 134

Container ships carry all kinds of goods in large metal boxes called containers. Cranes lift the containers off the ships and transfer them to trucks or trains.

Shipping

Millions of different products, from oil and bananas to books and computers, are transported around the world on cargo ships. Ships travel more slowly than planes, but they can carry a lot more goods at once and are much cheaper to use.

World travel

A century ago, if you wanted to travel across the sea, you had to go by boat. Huge ocean liners carried people around the world, and travel could take months.

Today, most people go long distances by plane, but boats such as ferries, hovercrafts and hydrofoils are still used for shorter distances. The only ocean liners left are cruise ships, which take people on long, relaxing sea journeys on vacations.

Sea pollution

The seas and oceans are huge and can absorb and break down a lot of the waste we pump into them. For example, a lot of sewage (waste from drains and toilets) goes into the sea and is broken down naturally into harmless chemicals.

However, some waste and litter doesn't break down fast enough, and ends up polluting the seas. Plastic, for example, dropped from ships or washed off beaches, can take up to 80 years to be broken down by the sea. Chemical and radioactive waste from factories, farms and nuclear power stations* can also end up in the sea and may poison plants, fish and other animals.

Oil tankers occasionally sink and spill the oil they are carrying. It can harm plants and animals, such as this seabird, by poisoning them or by coating them in oil so that they cannot breathe or move properly.

*Nuclear power, 25

Stalactites and stalagmites in the Cave of the Winds, Colorado Springs, USA.

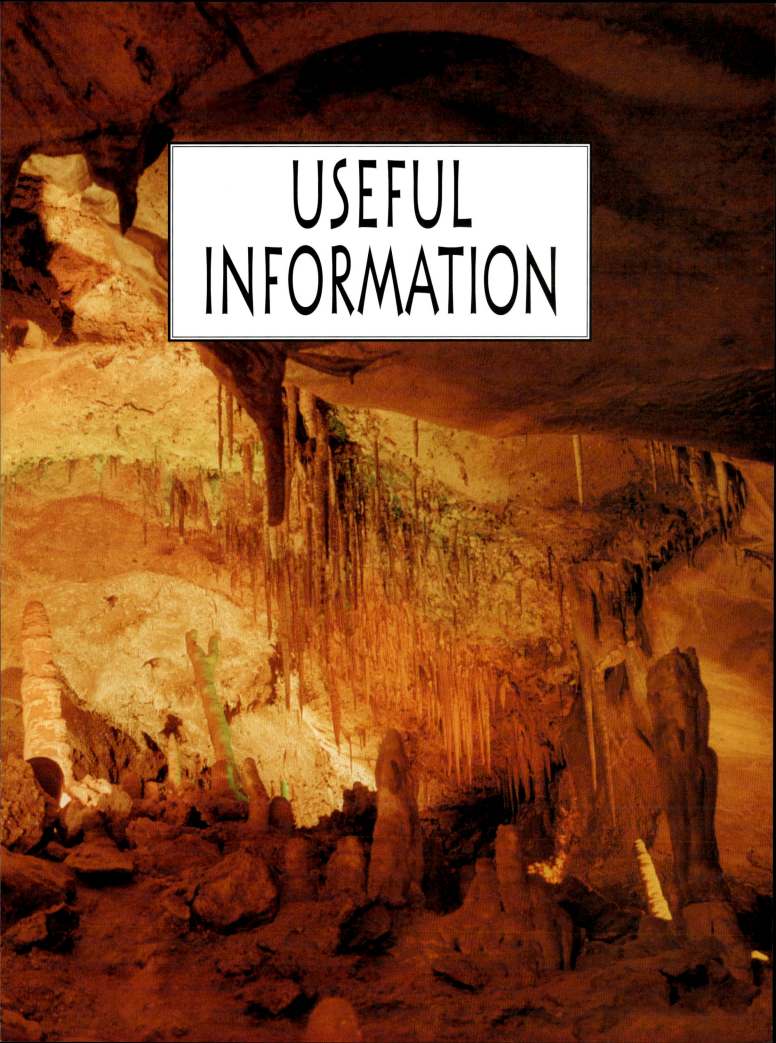

USEFUL INFORMATION

GLOSSARY

This glossary explains some of the words you may come across when reading about the Earth. Words in *italic type* have their own entry elsewhere in the glossary.

ablation zone The lower end of a *glacier*, where the ice melts and flows into streams and rivers, or into the sea.

abyssal plain A huge, flat expanse of seabed that forms most of the ocean floor.

accumulation zone The top of a *glacier*, where snow falls and is gradually compacted into ice.

acid rain Rain containing dissolved chemicals from polluted air. The chemicals make the water acidic, which means it can eat away at rock and damage plant life.

active volcano A volcano that might *erupt* at any time.

adaptation The way a plant or animal *species* develops over time to suit its *habitat*.

anticyclone An area of high *atmospheric pressure*, which pushes winds outward. It is the opposite of a *cyclone*.

aquifer A layer of *porous* rock that can hold water and carry it along under the ground.

arable Arable land is suitable for growing crops (plants). Arable farming means crop farming.

asteroid A small rock that *orbits* the Sun. There are thousands of asteroids in the part of the *Solar System* known as the Asteroid Belt.

atmosphere A layer of gases that surrounds the Earth and some other planets and stars.

atmospheric pressure The force the *atmosphere* exerts on Earth. It can change according to how warm the air is and how high you are above sea level.

atom A tiny particle. All *elements* are made up of atoms.

aurora Flickering lights, caused by *magnetic* particles from the Sun, that sometimes appear in the sky near the poles. The lights in the north are named the aurora borealis and those in the south are the aurora australis.

axis An imaginary line running through the middle of the Earth, from the *North Pole* to the *South Pole*, around which the Earth spins.

bacterium (plural: **bacteria**) A tiny *organism* found in the soil, in the air, and in plants and animals.

bedrock The solid layer of rock that lies underneath the soil, covering the Earth's surface.

biome An area with a *climate* that supports a particular range of plants and animals. For example, deserts, mountains and seas are all biomes.

black smoker A *hydrothermal vent* that churns out black water containing many dissolved minerals. The minerals gradually build up around the vent, forming a chimney.

camouflage Patterns or features, that help plants and animals to look like their backgrounds and avoid being seen. For example, a tiger's stripes blend in with long grass.

canopy The thick upper layer of leaves and branches in a rainforest.

carnivore An animal or plant that feeds on animals.

chlorofluorocarbon (CFC) Any of various chemicals that are thought to damage the layer of *ozone* in the Earth's *atmosphere*.

chlorophyll A green chemical in plants which enables them to convert sunlight into food.

climate The typical or average weather conditions in a particular region.

comet A chunk of dirty ice mixed with dust and grit which travels around the *Sun*.

community The group of plants and animals that live together in a particular *habitat*.

compass A device containing a *magnetic* needle that points to the *North Pole*. A compass is used to find your direction.

conservation Protecting and preserving *environments*, including the plants, animals and buildings that form a part of them, and trying to reduce the damage caused to them by *pollution*.

constellation A group of *stars* that form a recognizable pattern.

continent One of the Earth's major land masses.

continental crust Part of the Earth's *crust* that forms land masses. Continental crust is made mostly of a rock called granite and similar light rocks.

continental shelf A wide shelf of seabed that surrounds most land masses, making the sea much shallower near the land than it is in the middle of the oceans.

continental slope The steep slope leading from the edge of the *continental shelf* down to the deeper seabed.

coral reef A structure made up of the skeletons of small sea animals called coral polyps. A reef builds up gradually as old polyps die and new ones grow on top.

core The central part of the inside of the Earth, which scientists think is made of the metals iron and nickel.

Coriolis effect The effect of the spinning of the Earth, which forces winds and *currents* into a spiral.

crevasse A crack in a *glacier*.

crop rotation Changing the crop grown on a particular piece of land each year, to give the soil the opportunity to recover.

crust The Earth's solid outer layer. It consists of *continental crust* which forms the land, and *oceanic crust* which forms the seabed.

current A body of water or air which moves in a definite direction, often through a stiller surrounding body. For example, the Gulf Stream is a current that carries warm water across the Atlantic Ocean from the Caribbean to northern Europe.

cyclone An area of low *atmospheric pressure* where winds rotate inward.

debris Any kind of loose rock, mud or other matter – such as the rocks carried along by a *glacier*, or the material carried and deposited by a flowing river.

deforestation Reducing or removing forests by cutting down or burning trees. Soil is washed away more easily in deforested areas.

degree One 360th of a circle. Degrees are used with *latitude* and *longitude* to measure distance on the Earth's surface. One degree is one 360th of the distance around the Earth.

delta A fan-shaped system of streams, created when a river splits up into many smaller branches and deposits *debris* as it nears the sea.

deposition Dropping or leaving behind rocks or other *debris*.

desertification The process of non-desert land becoming desert.

dormant volcano A volcano that is temporarily inactive, but could *erupt* in the future. The word dormant means "sleeping".

drumlin A small hill formed from *debris* deposited by a moving *glacier*, lengthened in the direction of the movement of the glacier to form an oval shape.

dyke A barrier built at the coast to stop the sea from flooding the land at high *tide*.

ecosystem A living system that includes a group of plants and animals and the *habitat* they live in.

element A substance, such as iron, oxygen or silicon, made of one type of *atom*. There are over a hundred elements on Earth.

El Niño A weather phenomenon that sometimes makes part of the Pacific Ocean get much warmer than normal, causing severe storms.

emergent A tree that rises above the main *canopy* in a rainforest.

environment Surroundings, including the landscape, living things and the *atmosphere*.

Equator An imaginary line around the middle of the Earth, exactly halfway between the *North Pole* and the *South Pole*.

erratic A large boulder that has been deposited by a *glacier* and is left standing away from its source.

eruption The ejection of *lava*, rocks, hot ash and gases from a volcano.

estuary A wide channel that forms where a river joins the sea.w

evolution The gradual development of plants and animals, over many generations, to fit in better with their *habitats*.

exfoliation A process which involves shedding layers. When a rock exfoliates, its outer layers peel off like the layers of an onion. This is caused by changes in temperature, which make rock shrink and expand.

extinction The death of a *species* of plant or animal.

extinct volcano A volcano that has stopped being *active* or *dormant* and is not expected to *erupt* again.

fallow Fallow land is farmland that is being left to rest and recover between crops.

famine A widespread shortage of food, which can lead to starvation and the spread of diseases.

fault A crack in the Earth's *crust*.

fault creep The gradual movement of two pieces of the Earth's *crust* along a *fault*.

fertile Fertile land is land that is good for growing plants. Fertile also means able to reproduce.

fertilizer A substance, such as manure, that contains *nitrates* and other chemicals and is put on land to make it more *fertile*.

fold mountains A mountain range formed by the Earth's *crust* buckling up into folds when the *plates* of the crust push together.

food chain A sequence showing which *species* eat which.

food web A network of *food chains* showing which *species* eat each other in an *ecosystem*.

fossil The shape or remains of a plant or animal that died long ago, hardened and preserved in rock.

fossil fuel A fuel, such as coal, oil or gas, made from the compressed bodies of plants and animals that died many years ago.

freeze-thaw action The action of water that seeps into cracks in rocks and then freezes, which makes it expand. This expansion forces the cracks apart, so they gradually get bigger.

fungus (plural: **fungi**) A type of *organism*, including mushrooms, that is similar to a plant but has no leaves or flowers.

galaxy A huge group of stars and planets. There are millions of galaxies in the universe.

geostationary Moving in such a way as to remain above the same point on the Earth's surface. For example, geostationary *satellites* orbit the Earth at the same speed as the Earth spins, so they always stay above the same part of the Earth.

geyser A spring that discharges water and steam, heated up inside the Earth, in bursts.

glacial valley A deep U-shaped valley carved by a flowing *glacier*, left behind after the glacier melts.

glacier A mass of ice that flows very slowly downhill.

global warming The gradual warming-up of the Earth's atmosphere, possibly due to the *greenhouse effect*.

gorge A deep, narrow valley, shaped by a river gradually cutting down into the land it flows across.

gravity The pulling force that holds the *atmosphere* and objects in place on the Earth and stops them from floating out into space.

greenhouse effect The effect of certain gases in the *atmosphere* which trap heat from the Sun, causing the Earth to heat up.

greenhouse gas A gas, such as carbon dioxide, which contributes to the *greenhouse effect*.

groundwater Water that has soaked into the ground and is stored inside *porous* rock.

habitat The place where an animal or plant *species* lives.

hanging valley A valley found high up the side of a *glacial valley*. Hanging valleys once contained mini-glaciers that flowed into a large glacier. When glaciers melt, hanging valleys are left behind, high up the mountainside.

heat expansion The increase in size of many substances, such as wood or rock, as they get warmer.

hemisphere Half of the Earth. For example, the northern and southern hemispheres are separated by the *Equator*.

herbivore A animal that eats plants

horizon The line where you can see the land meeting the sky when you look into the distance. In soil science, it means a layer in the soil.

hot spot An area of the Earth's *crust* where *magma* breaks through and forms a volcano.

hot spring See **thermal spring.**

humidity The amount of water contained in the air.

hydroelectric power (HEP) Power created from the energy of flowing water.

hydrothermal vent A hole in the seabed, through which a *thermal spring* emerges. See also **black smoker.**

ice age A period when the Earth was much colder than average. There have been several major ice ages since the Earth began.

iceberg A huge chunk of a *glacier* that has broken off into the sea.

ice sheet A sheet of ice covering a large area, such as the ice that covers Antarctica. An ice sheet is a type of large *glacier* which flows outward from the middle.

igneous rock Rock formed when *magma* escapes from inside the Earth, and then cools and hardens.

impermeable Not allowing water to pass through.

infrared A type of energy that *radiates* from hot things. It is invisible to the human eye, but can be detected by infrared cameras.

intensive farming A type of farming that involves using chemicals and technology to increase *yield*.

interglacial A period of time within an *ice age* when the climate gets slightly warmer for a while.

International Date Line An imaginary line on the Earth's surface, to the east of which the date is one day earlier than to the west. It runs on the opposite side of the world to the *Prime Meridian Line* at 180° of *longitude*, except where it bends to avoid time change in populated areas.

irrigation The artificial watering of land to help grow crops.

isobar A line that links points with the same *atmospheric pressure*. The isobars on a weather map show patterns of atmospheric pressure.

landslide A sudden slippage of rocks and soil down a hillside, usually caused by heavy rain or earthquakes.

latitude A measurement of how many *degrees* a place is north or south of the *Equator*. Lines of latitude are imaginary lines around the Earth, parallel to the *Equator*.

lava Hot molten rock which bursts or flows out of volcanoes. Lava also sometimes seeps out of holes in the ground, called vents.

leap year A year every four years that has 366 days instead of 365. The extra day is added in February, to make February 29th.

longitude A measurement of how many *degrees* a place is east or west of the *Prime Meridian Line*. Lines of longitude are imaginary lines that run around the Earth from north to south.

magma Hot, molten rock inside the Earth.

magnet An object with magnetic force, an invisible force that attracts iron and steel. The ends of a magnet are known as its poles.

magnetic poles The Earth is like a giant *magnet*, and the ends of this magnet are called the magnetic poles. They move gradually over time, and are not in exactly the same place as the geographic *North Pole* and *South Pole*.

malaria A disease, affecting millions of people, which is spread by insects called mosquitoes.

mantle The thick layer of rock under the Earth's *crust*. Some of it is solid and some is *magma*.

manure Animal dung that can be used as a *fertilizer*.

meander A bend or long loop in a river. Meanders form when rivers flow across gently sloping land.

Mediterranean A type of *climate* that has warm winters and hot summers, and is good for growing many types of crops. It is named after the region around the Mediterranean Sea, but is also found in other parts of the world.

megacity A name for a city that has more than ten million people.

mestizo A Spaniard or Portuguese person of mixed origin, especially with Native American ancestors.

metamorphic rock Rock that has been changed by heat or pressure. For example, when a rock called shale is squashed, it hardens into a type of metamorphic rock called slate.

Middle East Part of Asia between the Red Sea and Persian Gulf, as well as Israel, Jordan, Syria, Lebanon, Iraq and Iran.

migration Moving from one place to another. Many animals migrate each season to find food.

mineral A non-living substance found in the Earth, such as salt, iron, diamond or quartz.

mirage An image of something that is somewhere else, caused by light bending in the *atmosphere*.

molecule Two or more *atoms* bonded together.

monsoon A strong seasonal change in the weather that affects certain parts of Asia. Monsoon regions have three seasons – a long, cool, dry season, a hot, humid season and a rainy season.

moon A natural *satellite* that *orbits* a *planet*. The Earth has one moon which orbits it once a month.

moraine Boulders, clay and other *debris* left behind by a *glacier*.

natural selection The theory that those animals and plants that are best suited to their *environment* are the most likely to survive.

New World A phrase used to mean North, Central and South America. The term was first applied by European explorers.

niche A particular plant or animal *species'* place in an *ecosystem*.

nitrate Any of a group of chemicals found in soil that helps plants grow.

northern lights See **aurora**.

North Pole The most northern point on the Earth, and one end of the *axis* the Earth spins around.

nuclear power Energy produced by splitting *atoms* of a *radioactive element* called uranium.

oasis A *fertile* area in a desert, supplied by water from an *aquifer*.

oceanic crust Part of the Earth's *crust* that forms the seabed. Oceanic crust is made mostly of a rock called basalt.

oceanic ridge A raised ridge on the seabed, caused by the *plates* of the Earth's *crust* pulling apart and *magma* pushing up in between.

oceanic trench A deep trench in the seabed that forms where one *plate* pushes underneath another.

omnivore An animal that eats both meat and plants. Omnivore means "everything-eater".

open cast mine A mine where minerals are extracted from near the surface, without digging tunnels or wells.

orbit The path of an object as it travels around, or orbits, another.

ore Rock containing metal that can be extracted.

organic farming A type of farming that doesn't use artificial chemicals and methods.

organic food Food produced by organic farming that contains no artificial chemicals.

organism A living thing, such as a plant, animal or *bacterium*.

outback The remote bush country of Australia.

outcrop An area of land where part of a rock formation reaches the surface.

oxbow lake A curved lake left behind when a river *meander* gets cut off from the rest of the river.

ozone A type of oxygen in which each *molecule* contains three oxygen *atoms* instead of two.

ozone layer A layer of *ozone* in the Earth's *atmosphere*, 20–50km (12–30 miles) above the Earth's surface, which protects the Earth from the *Sun's* rays. The ozone layer may be being damaged by *chlorofluorocarbons*.

Pangaea The name scientists give to a huge continent that they think once existed on Earth. It gradually broke up to form the *continents* we have today.

pastoral farming A type of farming that involves raising and breeding animals.

permafrost A layer of the ground that is permanently frozen.

photosynthesis A chemical process in plants, which converts sunlight into food.

planet A celestial body that *orbits* a *star*. For example, Earth and Mars are planets which orbit the *Sun*.

plate One of the large pieces of *lithosphere* that make up the Earth's surface layer.

plate tectonics The theory that *plates* gradually move around and rub against each other.

poles The *North Pole* and the *South Pole*, the coldest points of the Earth and those farthest from the *Equator*.

pollution Waste or dirt, such as exhaust from cars, that builds up faster than it can be broken down.

population The number of people living in a particular place.

porous rock Rock that can soak up water like a sponge and store it underground.

port A town or city where ships can load and unload.

precipitation Rain, snow, hail or any other water falling from the sky.

Prime Meridian Line An imaginary line that runs from north to south through Greenwich, England, at zero *degrees* of *longitude*. The time along the Prime Meridian Line is called Greenwich Mean Time.

projection A representation of the Earth's surface on a flat map.

radar A system that detects objects such as clouds by sending out radio waves and collecting the signals that bounce back. Radar stands for **RA**dio **D**etecting **A**nd **R**anging.

radiation Energy, such as light, heat or *radioactive* particles, that radiates (flows outward) from an energy source. For example, the *Sun* radiates light and heat.

radioactive A substance that gives out *radiation*. Radioactive substances, such as uranium, give off particles which can be harmful.

remote-operated vehicle or **ROV** A remote-controlled robot used for exploring the seabed.

remote sensing Recording information from a long distance away; for example, measuring sea temperatures from a *satellite*.

rift valley A valley formed on land where two *plates* of the Earth's *crust* pull away from each other.

Ring of Fire A group of volcanoes and *faults* that forms a huge ring in the Pacific Ocean.

satellite An object that *orbits* a *planet*. Satellites are built to do jobs such as monitoring the weather.

scale The size of a map in relation to the area it represents. If a map's scale is 1:100, 1cm on the map represents 100cm of the area shown.

sedimentary rock Rock made up of particles of sand, mud and other *debris* that have settled on the seabed and been squashed down to form hard rock.

selective breeding Developing plants and animals by choosing those with good qualities for farming.

sewage Waste and dirty water from sinks and bathrooms.

shanty town A makeshift town on the outskirts of a city where people build their own homes out of waste materials.

slash-and-burn A method of destroying trees quickly to make room for farmland.

smog A mixture of smoke and fog

Solar System The *Sun* and the *planets, satellites* and other objects that *orbit* it.

solar year The amount of time it takes the Earth to *orbit* the *Sun* once. A solar year is 365.26 days.

sonar A method of bouncing sounds off objects and measuring the results in order to make maps. Sonar is used to map the seabed.

South Pole The most southern point on the Earth, and one end of the *axis* the Earth spins around.

species (plural: **species**) A type of plant, animal or other living thing.

stalactite A column of stone hanging down inside a cave, made by water dripping from the roof and depositing dissolved minerals.

stalagmite A tower of stone rising from the ground in a cave, made by water dripping onto the floor and depositing dissolved minerals.

star A huge ball of burning gas in space. The *Sun*, in the middle of our *Solar System*, is a star.

stoma (plural: **stomata**) One of the tiny holes in the leaves of plants. A stoma allows gases and water in and out. See also **transpiration**.

stratum (plural: **strata**) A layer of rock.

subduction zone An area of the seabed where one *plate* of the Earth's *lithosphere* plunges beneath another, forming a deep trench.

submersible A small submarine used by scientists to explore the oceans and the seabed.

subsoil A layer of rough soil underneath the *topsoil*. The rocks and cracks in subsoil help water to drain through it.

Sun The medium-sized *star* that lies in the middle of our *Solar System*.

temperate A type of *climate* that is mild and damp.

terrace One of a series of large steps dug into hillsides to hold soil and water in place for farming.

tertiary industry An industry, such as teaching or banking, that provides services for others.

thermal spring A flow of water heated by underground rocks that emerges on the Earth's surface. Also known as a hot spring.

tide The daily rise and fall of the sea, caused by the Moon's *gravity*.

time zone A region where the same standard time is used.

topsoil The rich, uppermost layer of soil. It contains *humus* and *organisms* that make it *fertile*.

transpiration A process where water that has been sucked in through a plant's roots travels up to the leaves, and transpires, or evaporates, through the *stomata*.

treeline The height up a mountain above which there are no more trees (because it is too cold and windy for them to survive).

tributary A river that flows into a bigger river, instead of into the sea.

tropics The warm, wet areas on either side of the *Equator*, between the Tropics of Cancer and Capricorn.

tsunami A giant wave caused by an earthquake, landslide or volcanic activity on the seabed.

tundra A type of land, found in the Arctic, where a layer of the ground is permanently frozen.

turbine A machine that converts turning power (such as the spinning of a waterwheel) into electricity.

ultraviolet (UV) A type of invisible *radiation* from the Sun which can cause skin damage.

understorey The level of a rainforest where small trees and plants grow, between the *canopy* and the forest floor.

water table The top level of *groundwater* that is stored in underground rock.

yield The amount of food or other produce that is grown on a particular piece of land.

MAPS AND LINES

The Earth is a huge, round ball of rock moving through space. It has no "top" or "bottom" and no lines marked on it. Lines such as the Equator, the Arctic Circle and the International Date Line, which are explained here, are all imaginary. They are used to help us measure distances and find places on maps.

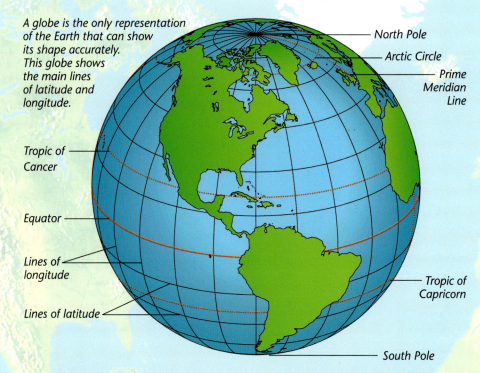

A globe is the only representation of the Earth that can show its shape accurately. This globe shows the main lines of latitude and longitude.

What do the lines mean?

• **Lines of latitude**, or **parallels**, run around the globe, dividing it into flat slices. Lines of latitude get shorter the closer they are to the poles, but they never meet each other.

• The **Equator** is the biggest and most important line of latitude. It runs around the globe halfway between the North Pole and the South Pole. The other lines of latitude are measured north and south from it.

• **Lines of longitude**, also known as **meridians**, run from the North Pole to the South Pole, dividing the globe into segments, like the segments of an orange. They all meet at the North Pole and at the South Pole.

• The **Prime Meridian Line** is the most important line of longitude, because all the other lines are measured from it. But it is not longer than any of the others; the lines are all the same size. It was decided in 1884 that the Prime Meridian would run through Greenwich, near London in England.

• **Degrees** (°) are used to measure distance on the globe. One degree is one 360th of the way around the globe. Lines of latitude are measured in degrees north and south of the Equator, while lines of longitude are measured in degrees east and west of the Prime Meridian Line. For example, somewhere that is 50°S and 100°E has a latitude 50 degrees south of the Equator, and a longitude 100 degrees east of the Prime Meridian Line.

• **Minutes** (′) and **seconds** (″) are smaller distances, used for making more precise measurements. There are 60 minutes in one degree, and 60 seconds in one minute.

• The **Arctic Circle** is a line of latitude at 66°30′ north. The area north of it includes the North Pole and is known as the **Arctic**.

• The **Antarctic Circle** is a line of latitude at 66°30′ south. It contains the South Pole and the area south of it is known as the **Antarctic**.

• The **tropics** are two lines of latitude near the Equator. The **Tropic of Cancer** is at 23°27′ north and the **Tropic of Capricorn** is at 23°27′ south. The hot, stormy area that lies between these two lines is also sometimes known as the **tropics**.

• The **International Date Line** is near the 180th meridian (the line at 180° longitude, directly opposite the Prime Meridian Line). It runs mostly through the Pacific Ocean, and is not straight but bends to avoid the land. It is part of the system that is used to define international time zones (see opposite). The date changes from one side of the line to the other.

Map projections

A flat map cannot show the world as it really is. So, to represent the round Earth on a flat surface, it has to be distorted (stretched) or divided into pieces. Some methods of doing this, called projections, are shown here.

- A **cylindrical projection** is similar to what you would get if you wrapped a piece of paper around a globe to form a cylinder, then shone a light inside the globe. The shapes of the countries would be projected onto the paper. Near the Equator they would be accurate, but near the poles they would look distorted.

A cylindrical map projection

- In the **Robinson projection**, the longitude lines curve in at the poles, so countries in the far north and south don't look too big. The curved lines can be confusing, but the map represents the Earth's proportions quite well.

The Robinson map projection

- The **Peters projection** stretches the countries near to the Equator, so that all the countries are the right size in relation to each other. But this makes them look too long, so they aren't the right shape.

The Peters map projection

- The **Homolosine projection** splits the globe up into sections. It makes each country almost the right shape and size, but it's not very useful for working out distances and routes, especially if you live near one of the edges!

The Homolosine map projection

- The **Mercator projection** is probably the most well-known projection. It was invented by Gerardus Mercator in 1538. It is like a cylindrical projection, but is stretched out at the poles. The countries are the right shape, but those nearest the poles look too big.

The Mercator map projection

Time zones

Because the sun rises and sets at different times across the world, the Earth is divided into 24 time zones. In each zone, people set their clocks to their own standard time. There is a new zone every 15 degrees of longitude, but this is only a rough guide, as whole countries or states usually keep to the same local time instead of sticking to the zones exactly. In some countries, they use a different Summer Time. This map shows how the time zones work. The zones are measured in hours ahead of or behind Greenwich Mean Time, or GMT, which is the time at the Prime Meridian Line.

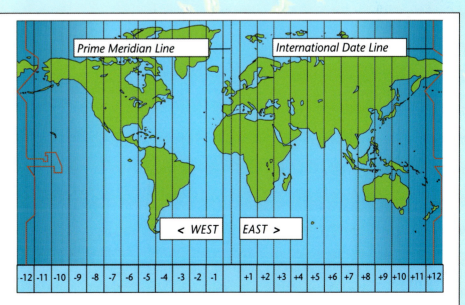

This diagram shows the 24 time zones. The areas ahead of GMT meet the areas behind GMT at the International Date Line (on the opposite side of the world from the Prime Meridian Line). If you travel east across the International Date Line, you go back 24 hours. If you travel west across it, you go forward 24 hours.

THE EARTH'S CYCLES

The Earth is constantly going through repeated processes, or cycles, such as the orbit of the Earth around the Sun, the way it spins and tilts as it moves through space, the orbit of the Moon around the Earth, and the sequence of the tides.

Days and years

Days and years are created by the movement of the Earth in relation to the Sun. Here are some facts and figures about the Earth's orbit.

• One **day** is the amount of time it takes the Earth to spin around on its axis. We divide each day into 24 hours of 60 minutes each.

• The exact amount of time it takes the Earth to make one complete orbit around the Sun is 365.26 days. This is known as a **solar year**.

• Instead of having 365.26 days, a normal **year** on Earth has exactly 365 days (because this is easier for us). Every four years another day is added to make up the difference. A year with an extra day in it is called a **leap year**. The extra day is added to February, so in leap years February has 29 days instead of 28.

• Making every fourth year a leap year does not even things out exactly, so some leap years are missed. Usually, every fourth year is a leap year, such as 1988, 1992 and 1996. But century years, such as 1700, 1800 and 1900, are not leap years. However, millennium years, such as the year 2000, *are* leap years.

Calendars

A **calendar** is a system of measuring years, months, weeks and days. People don't all agree when the world began, so years cannot be measured from then. Several different calendars, mostly based on religious beliefs, are used today.

Years ago	Christian calendar	Islamic calendar	Chinese calendar	Hebrew calendar
5,800				
5,600				This is when Jews believe the world began.
5,400				
5,200				
5,000				
4,800				
4,600				
4,400			Emperor Huang Di is said to have invented the Chinese calendar 4,600 years ago.	
4,200				
4,000				
3,800				
3,600				
3,400				
3,200				
3,000				
2,800				
2,600				
2,400				
2,200				
2,000				
1,800	The Christian calendar begins with the birth of Jesus Christ.			
1,600				
1,400		This is when the Prophet Muhammad fled from Mecca to Medina.		
1,200				
1,000				
800				
600				
400				
200				
0				

This chart shows how many years ago the different calendars began. When the Christian calendar is on the year 2000, the Islamic calendar is on the year 1378, and so on.

The Moon

A **moon** is a ball of rock orbiting (moving around) a planet. The Earth only has one moon, but some planets have more. Saturn, for example, has at least 30 moons.

Our Moon orbits the Earth once every 27 days, 7 hours and 43 minutes. The Moon "shines" because it is reflecting light from the Sun. Whether we see a full moon, a thin crescent moon, or something in between, depends on what position the Moon is in and how much sunlight it can reflect onto the Earth. These different shapes are called the phases of the Moon.

Phases of the Moon

- A **new moon** does not shine at all. The Moon's cycle begins when the Moon is between the Earth and the Sun, so none of the light it reflects can reach the Earth.

- The Moon's **first** and **last quarters** are when it has moved a quarter or three quarters of the way around its cycle and is alongside the Earth. We see half of it reflecting the Sun.

- A **full moon** is what you see when the Moon is on the opposite side of the Earth from the Sun. You can then see sunlight reflecting off the whole of the surface facing Earth.

More Moon facts

- When the Moon is moving away from the Sun and growing fuller, it is **waxing**. When it moves around toward the Sun again and seems to be getting smaller, it is **waning**.

- A **crescent moon** is between a new moon and a half moon, and looks like a crescent or C-shape.

- A **gibbous moon** is between a half moon and a full moon, and is a fat oval shape.

- A **lunar month** is the amount of time it takes the Moon to complete its cycle: 29 days, 12 hours and 44 minutes. This is longer than the orbit time, because while the Moon is making its orbit around the Earth, the Earth is moving around the Sun and so changing its own position.

- Like the Earth, the Moon spins around on its axis. It does this every 27 days, 7 hours and 43 minutes. This is exactly the same amount of time as the time it takes to travel around the Earth, which means we always see the same side of the Moon from Earth. However, we can see the other side of the Moon in pictures taken by spacecraft.

- The Moon is 3,476km (2,160 miles) across, about a quarter of the width of the Earth. Its circumference is 10,927km (6,790 miles) and its distance away from the Earth varies between 356,399 and 384,403km (221,456 and 238,857 miles). It orbits the Earth at about 3,700kph (2,300mph).

- A **month** on Earth is a period of time based on the Moon's cycle. But to make 12 months fit into a year, an average month is about 30 days long, slightly longer than a lunar month.

- A **blue moon** happens when there are two full moons within one Earth month. The second full moon of the two is called the blue moon.

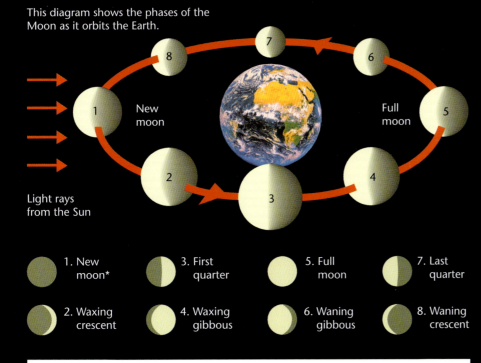

This diagram shows the phases of the Moon as it orbits the Earth.

Light rays from the Sun

1. New moon*
2. Waxing crescent
3. First quarter
4. Waxing gibbous
5. Full moon
6. Waning gibbous
7. Last quarter
8. Waning crescent

Tides

The water in the Earth's seas and oceans rises and falls twice a day. These movements are called tides, and they are caused by the gravity of the Moon.

As the Earth spins, different parts of its surface move past the Moon. The part nearest the Moon has a high tide, when the water rises as the Moon pulls it.

At the same time, a high tide also happens on the opposite side of the Earth, because of a reaction called centrifugal force, created by the way the Earth and the Moon move around each other.

While this is happening, there is a low tide on the parts of the Earth's surface that are not facing or opposite the Moon. Each part of the world has two high tides and two low tides every day.

*This is how Moon phases look from the northern hemisphere. From the southern hemisphere, the sequence is reversed, so that a southern waxing Moon looks like a northern waning Moon. From the Equator, a crescent Moon may look like a U or an n.

GEOGRAPHERS AND SCIENTISTS

Geography is the scientific study of the Earth. *Geo* is Greek for "Earth", and "graphy" comes from the Greek "graphein", which means "to write". Sciences that relate to the Earth are known as Earth sciences or geosciences.

Many geographers and scientists are involved in studying different aspects of the Earth. The table below lists some of these areas of study, the scientists and geographers who study them and the area each one deals with.

Name of study	Name of scientist/geographer	What is it?
Biogeography	Biogeographer	The study of the distribution of plants and animals
Geography	Geographer	The study of the Earth's features and processes, climates, resources and the way people relate to the Earth
Historical geography	Historical geographer	The geographic study of a place or region at a specific time in the past, or the study of geographic change over a period of time
Regional geography	Regional geographer	The study of the interrelationship between human and physical geography in a particular region
Urban geography	Urban geographer	The geographical study of cities
Geology	Geologist	The study of planet Earth, what it is made of, how it formed and how it is changing
Mineralogy	Mineralogist	The study of minerals
Geomorphology	Geomorphologist	The study of landforms (the shapes and features on the Earth's surface) and the processes which cause them
Volcanology	Volcanologist	The study of volcanoes
Seismology	Seismologist	The study of earthquakes and earth tremors
Oceanography	Oceanographer	The study of seas and oceans and the seabed
Meteorology	Meteorologist	The study of the weather and weather forecasting
Climatology	Climatologist	The study of climates past and present
Ecology	Ecologist	The study of the relationship between living things (including humans) and their surroundings on Earth
Pedology	Pedologist	The study of soil, which is also often known as soil science
Cartography	Cartographer	The science of designing and making maps, and collecting the information needed to make them

These are some of the famous scientists and geographers who have contributed to our understanding of how the Earth and its processes work, and explored other aspects of geography.

al-Idrisi (c.1100–c.1165)
Arabic geographer and author who explored the Mediterranean region, created an early map of the world, and wrote a book, *The Book of Roger*, describing his travels.

Aristotle (384BC–322BC)
Greek scientist and philosopher who wrote on many subjects. He realized that the Earth was a sphere, although it took a long time for everyone to accept this. (Until about AD1500, many people still thought the world was flat.)

Darwin, Charles (1809–1882)
English scientist who developed the theory of natural selection, which argues that plant and animal species change, or evolve, over long periods of time. This theory was controversial, partly because it suggested that the Earth was much older than many people believed.

Davis, William Morris (1850–1934) American geologist and meteorologist who founded the science of geomorphology. He developed a theory of how the process of erosion forms a cycle and was famous for his detailed diagrams showing how features of the Earth's crust are formed.

Democritus (c.460BC–c.370BC)
Greek philosopher who was the first to claim that all matter was made up of tiny particles, or atoms. He also studied earthquakes, volcanoes, the water cycle and erosion.

Eratosthenes (c.276BC–c.196BC)
Greek scientist and geographer who made the first measurement of the distance around the Earth, using the stars as a guide. He was the first person to use the word *geography*.

Gould, Stephen Jay (1941–2002)
American geologist and paleontologist (person who studies fossils) who built on the theories of Charles Darwin. He wrote many popular books, such as *Wonderful Life* (1989).

Hartshorne, Richard (1899–1992)
A leading American philosopher of geography. His major work was *Perspective on the Nature of Geography*, published in 1939, in which he argued for the study of specific places and regions.

Henry the Navigator (1394–1460)
A prince of Portugal who planned and paid for many journeys of exploration to Africa. He opened a school which taught explorers how to navigate (find their way) and record their discoveries.

Herodotus (c.484BC–c.425BC)
Greek historian known as the "father of history", but also regarded as the founder of geography because he was the first person to put historical events in a geographical setting.

Humboldt, Alexander von (1769–1859)
German explorer who contributed to geography, geology, meteorology and oceanography. He explored South America and wrote *Kosmos* (The Cosmos), in 1844, describing the geography and geology of the world.

Hutton, James (1726–1797)
Scottish scientist who studied rocks and minerals, and is sometimes called "the father of geology". He said that the Earth's crust changed gradually through erosion, volcanic eruptions and other processes.

Kant, Immanual (1724–1804)
Famous German philosopher who taught physical geography.

Lyell, Sir Charles (1797–1875)
Scottish geologist who developed the theories of James Hutton. He was also a friend of Charles Darwin and his ideas helped Darwin with his theory of natural selection.

Mackinder, Sir Halford J. (1861–1947)
Leading British geographer in the early 20th century. He was head of the first university geography department in the United Kingdom.

Ptolemy (c.AD100–c.AD170)
Egyptian geographer and astronomer. He devised an early system of latitude and longitude and used it to create many maps.

Ritter, Carl (1779–1859)
German geographer who was the first professor of geography at Berlin University. He wrote his major work, the 19-volume *Erdkunde* (Earth Science), in 1817 and is seen as the founder of modern regional geography.

Strabo (c.64BC–c.AD20)
Greek historian and geographer. He wrote *Geography*, a 17-volume book which provides geographical information on the Roman Empire.

Varenius, Bernhardus (1622–1650)
Dutch geographer. He wrote a major book, *Geographia Generalis* (General Geography) in 1650, in which he was one of the first people to distinguish between physical and human geography.

Wegener, Alfred (1880–1930)
German meteorologist who claimed that the Earth's continents were once joined together in one big continent, which he named Pangaea. His theories were not widely accepted until the 1960s when they were used to develop the theory of plate tectonics.

WORLD RECORDS

Here are some of the Earth's longest rivers, highest mountains and other amazing world records. But the world is always changing; mountains wear down, rivers change shape, and new buildings are constructed. Ways of measuring things can also change. That's why you may find slightly different figures in different books.

Highest mountains	
Everest, Nepal/China	8,848m (29,029ft)
K2, Pakistan/China	8,612m (28,253ft)
Kanchenjunga, India/Nepal	8,586m (28,169ft)
Lhotse, Nepal/China	8,516m (27,940ft)
Makalu, Nepal/China	8,462m (27,762ft)
Cho Oyu, Nepal/China	8,201m (26,906ft)
Dhaulagiri, Nepal	8,167m (26,795ft)
Manaslu, Nepal	8,156m (26,759ft)
Nanga Parbat, Pakistan	8,125m (26,658ft)
Annapurna, Nepal	8,091m (26,545ft)

Longest rivers	
Nile, Africa	6,671km (4,145 miles)
Amazon, South America	6,437km (4,000 miles)
Chang Jiang (Yangtze), China	6,380km (3,964 miles)
Mississippi/Missouri, USA	6,019km (3,740 miles)
Yenisey/Angara, Russia	5,539km (3,442 miles)
Huang He (Yellow), China	5,464km (3,395 miles)
Ob/Irtysh/Black Irtysh, Asia	5,411km (3,362 miles)
Parana/River Plate, S. America	4,880km (3,032 miles)
Congo, Africa	4,700km (2,920 miles)
Amur/Shilka/Onon, Asia	4,416km (2,744 miles)

Biggest natural lakes by surface area	
Caspian Sea	386,400 sq km (149,190 sq mi)
Lake Superior	82,100 sq km (31,700 sq mi)
Lake Victoria	69,484 sq km (26,828 sq mi)
Lake Huron	59,600 sq km (23,010 sq mi)
Lake Michigan	57,800 sq km (22,317 sq mi)
Lake Tanganyika	32,600 sq km (12,590 sq mi)
Lake Baikal	31,722 sq km (12,248 sq mi)
Great Bear Lake	31,153 sq km (12,028 sq mi)
Lake Nyasa	29,600 sq km (11,430 sq mi)
Great Slave Lake	28,568 sq km (11,030 sq mi)

Deepest ocean	
The Mariana Trench, part of the Pacific Ocean, is the deepest part of the sea at 10,920 meters (35,827ft) deep.	

Deepest lake	
Lake Baikal in Russia is the deepest lake in the world. At its deepest point it is 1,642m (5,387ft) deep.	

Biggest islands	
Greenland	2,130,800 sq km (822,706 sq mi)
New Guinea	785,753 sq km (303,381 sq mi)
Borneo	748,168 sq km (288,869 sq mi)
Madagascar	587,713 sq km (226,917 sq mi)
Baffin Island	507,451 sq km (195,928 sq mi)
Sumatra	443,066 sq km (171,069 sq mi)
Honshu	225,800 sq km (87,182 sq mi)
Victoria Island	217,291 sq km (83,897 sq mi)
Great Britain	209,331 sq km (80,823 sq mi)
Ellesmere Island	196,236 sq km (75,767 sq mi)

Tallest inhabited buildings	
Burj Khalifa, Dubai	828m (2,717ft)
Mecca Royal Clock Tower Hotel	601m (1,972ft)
One World Trade Center, New York	541.3m (1,776ft)
Taipei 101, Taipei	509m (1,670ft)
Shanghai WFC, Shanghai	492m (1,614ft)
ICC Tower, Hong Kong	484m (1,588ft)
Petronas Towers, Kuala Lumpur	452m (1,483ft)
Zifeng Tower, Nanjing	450m (1,476ft)
Willis (Sears) Tower, Chicago	442.1m (1,450ft)
Kingkey 100, Shenzhen	441.8m (1,449ft)

Biggest cities/urban areas	
Tokyo-Yokohama, Japan	37.8 million
Jakarta, Indonesia	30.5 million
Delhi, India	25.0 million
Manila, Philippines	24.1 million
Seoul-Incheon, South Korea	23.5 million
Shanghai, China	23.4 million
Karachi, Pakistan	22.1 million
Beijing, China	21.0 million
New York City, USA	20.6 million
Guangzhou-Foshan, China	20.6 million

Famous waterfalls	Height
Angel Falls, Venezuela	979m (3,212ft)
Mardalsfossen, Norway	645m (2,116ft)
Sutherland Falls, New Zealand	580m (1,903ft)
Jog Falls, India	253m (830ft)
Victoria Falls, Zimbabwe/Zambia	105m (344ft)
Iguacu Falls, Brazil/Argentina	82m (269ft)
Niagara Falls, Canada/USA	51m (167ft)

Natural disasters

Natural disasters can be measured in different ways. For example, some earthquakes score highly on the Richter scale, while others cause more destruction. The earthquakes, volcanic eruptions, floods, hurricanes and tornadoes listed here are among the most famous and destructive disasters in history.

Modern earthquakes	Richter scale	Deaths and other effects
San Francisco, USA, 1906	7.8	3,000; deadliest in USA; Great Fire
Haiyuan, China, 1920	7.8	200,000; towns totally destroyed
Tokyo-Kanto, Japan, 1923	7.9	142,807; caused Great Tokyo Fire
Ashgabat, Turkmenistan, 1948	7.3	110,000; capital city demolished
Valdivia, Chile, 1960	9.5	2,000; strongest recorded quake
Alaska, USA, 1964	9.2	128; strongest ever quake in USA
Tangshan, China, 1976	7.5	655,237; deadliest in 20th century
Indian Ocean, 2004	9.1	230,000; deadliest recorded tsunami
Haiti region, 2010	7.0	85–316,000; 1.3 million homeless
Tohoku, Japan, 2011	9.0	15,703; strongest in Japan; tsunami

Volcanic eruptions	Disastrous effects
Mount Vesuvius, Italy, AD79	Pompeii flattened; up to 20,000 died
Laki, Iceland, 1783	Huge lava flow; poison fog; famine; 9,350 died
Unzen, Japan, 1792	Over 15,000 died in landslide and tsunami
Tambora, Indonesia, 1815	92,000 people starved to death
Krakatau, Indonesia, 1883	36,500 drowned in resulting tsunami
Mount Pelee, Martinique, 1902	Nearly 30,000 people buried in ash flows
Kelut, Indonesia, 1919	Over 5,000 people drowned in hot mud
Mount St. Helens, USA, 1980	Only 61 died but a large area was destroyed
Ruiz, Colombia, 1985	25,000 people died in giant mud flows
Mt. Pinatubo, Philippines, 1991	847 killed by collapsing roofs and disease

Floods	Disastrous effects
Netherlands, 1287	Storm tide broke a dam, killing 80,000
China, 1887	900,000 died after the Yellow River flooded
Johnstown, USA, 1889	2,200 killed in a flood caused by rain
China, 1931	Many rivers flooded; 3.7 million people died
North Sea Flood, 1953	2,551 killed in Netherlands, UK and Belgium
Italy, 1963	Vaoint Dam overflowed; 2–3,000 killed
East Pakistan, 1970	Giant wave caused by cyclone killed 250,000
Bangladesh, 1988	1,300 died, 30m homeless in monsoon flood
Southern USA, 1993	$12bn of damage after Mississippi flooded
Venezuela, 1999	Mudslides in Vargas region killed 20,066

Storms	Disastrous effects
Caribbean "Great Hurricane", 1780	Biggest-ever hurricane, killed over 20,000
Galveston Hurricane, USA, 1900	Texas hit; 6–12,000 died; $100 bn of damage
Hong Kong typhoon, China, 1906	10,000 people died in this giant hurricane
Tri-State Tornado, USA, 1925	Up to 700 people died across three states
Hurricane Fifi, Honduras, 1974	8,000 people died and 100,000 left homeless
Hurricane Mitch, C. America, 1998	Over 11,000 killed across Central America
Hurricane Katrina, USA, 2005	Over 1,800 killed and $90 bn of damage

Amazing Earth facts

The Earth is 12,103km (7,520 miles) across. Its circumference (the distance around the Equator) is 38,022km (23,627 miles) and it is 149,503,000 km (92,897,000 miles) away from the Sun.

To make one complete orbit around the Sun, the Earth has to travel 938,900,000km (583,400,000 miles). To do this in just a year, it has to travel very fast. Because of the atmosphere surrounding the Earth, you can't feel it moving. But in fact you are zooming through space faster than any rocket.

- **Orbit speed** The Earth travels around the Sun at a speed of about 106,000kph (65,868mph).

- **Spinning speed** The Earth also spins around an axis, but the speed you are spinning at depends on where you live. Places on the Equator move at 1,600kph (995mph). New York moves at around 1,100kph (684mph). Near the poles, the spinning is not very fast at all. (You can see how this works by looking at a spinning globe.)

- **Solar System speed** The whole Solar System, including the Sun, the Earth and its moon, and the other planets and their moons, is moving at 72,400kph (45,000 mph) through the galaxy.

- **Galaxy speed** Our galaxy, the Milky Way, whizzes through the universe at a speed of 2,172,150kph (1,350,000mph).

MEASUREMENTS

Measuring things – distance, area, weight, volume, time and temperature – is one of the most important parts of science. There are three main systems of measurement: metric, and the near-identical UK imperial and US customary measurements. This page shows how each system works, and how to convert from one into the other.

UK imperial and US customary

These systems of measurement developed from traditional English units. They can be hard to use because they are not based on the decimal (base 10) system that we use for numbers. Abbreviations or symbols for some units are shown below in brackets. US and UK units are also marked if they are measured differently.

Length and distance
12 inches (in or ") = 1 foot (ft or ')
3 feet = 1 yard (yd)
1,760 yards = 1 mile
3 miles = 1 league

Area
144 square inches = 1 square foot
9 square feet = 1 square yard
4,840 square yards = 1 acre
640 acres = 1 square mile

Weight
16 drams (dr) = 1 ounce (oz)
16 ounces = 1 pound (lb)
14 pounds = 1 stone (st) (UK/Ireland)
2,240 pounds = 1 UK ton ("long ton")
2,000 pounds = 1 US ton ("short ton")

Volume and capacity
1,728 cubic inches = 1 cubic foot (ft³)
27 cubic feet = 1 cubic yard (yd³)
20 fluid ounces = 1 pint (pt) (UK)
16 fluid ounces = 1 liquid* pint (US)
2 pints = 1 quart (qt)
8 pints (4 quarts) = 1 gallon (gal)

*The USA also uses a (slightly larger) dry pint.

Temperature
The unit of temperature is one degree (°) Fahrenheit (F). The freezing point of water is 32°F and the boiling point of water is 212°F.

Metric

The metric or decimal system is based on the metre or meter, a unit of measurement which was first used in France in the 1790s. Metric units are multiples of each other by 10, 100 or 1,000. Countries around the world are gradually switching from imperial to metric. Many of the metric units have both US spellings (-er) and European spellings (-re).

Length and distance
10 millimeters/millimetres (mm) = 1 centimeter/centimetre (cm)
100 cm = 1 meter/metre (m)
1,000 m = 1 kilometer/kilometre (km)

Area
100 square mm (mm²) = 1 square cm (cm²)
10,000 square cm = 1 square m (m²)
10,000 square m = 1 hectare
1,000,000 square m = 1 square kilometer/kilometre (km²)

Weight
1,000 grams (g) = 1 kilogram (kg)
1,000 kilograms = 1 tonne (t)

Volume and capacity
1 cubic cm (cc or cm³) = 1 milliliter/millilitre (ml)
1,000 ml = 1 liter/litre (l)
1,000 l = 1 cubic m (m³)

Temperature
The metric temperature unit is one degree (°) Celsius (C). Water freezes at 0°C and boils at 100°C.

Conversion tables

To convert	into	multiply by
cm	inches	0.394
m	yards	1.094
km	miles	0.621
grams	ounces	0.035
kilograms	pounds	2.205
tonnes	tons (UK)	1.102
tonnes	tons (US)	0.984
square cm	square inches	0.155
square m	square yards	1.196
square km	square miles	0.386
hectares	acres	2.471
litres	pints (UK)	1.76
liters	liquid pints (US)	2.113
liters	dry pints (US)	1.816
To convert	**into**	**multiply by**
inches	cm	2.54
yards	m	0.914
miles	km	1.609
ounces	grams	28.35
pounds	kilograms	0.454
tons (US)	tonnes	1.12
tons (UK)	tonnes	1.016
square inches	square cm	6.452
square yards	square m	0.836
square miles	square km	2.59
acres	hectares	0.405
liquid pints (US)	liters	0.473
dry pints (US)	liters	0.551
pints (UK)	litres	0.568

USBORNE QUICKLINKS

This book contains descriptions of websites where you can find out more about the Earth. To visit the sites, go to the Usborne Quicklinks website at **www.usborne.com/quicklinks** and enter the keywords "planet earth".

What you can do

Here are some of the things you can do at the websites we recommend:

- Browse satellite images of Earth from space, from volcanic eruptions in Japan to dust storms in Africa

- Watch video clips of earthquakes, volcanoes and geysers

- Investigate global warming and find out more about weather and climate change

- Watch video clips about some of the most amazing animals on Earth

- Try test-yourself quizzes about rainforests, mountains, oceans and more

Downloadable pictures

Pictures marked with a ★ symbol in this book can be downloaded at the Usborne Quicklinks website and used in home or school projects. They must not be used for any commercial purpose.

Site availability

The websites described in this book are regularly checked and reviewed by Usborne editors and the links at Usborne Quicklinks are updated. If a website closes down, we will replace it with a new link. Sometimes we add extra links too. Please note that the content of a website may change at any time and Usborne Publishing isnot responsible for the content or availabilityof any website other than its own.

Internet safety

When using the internet, children should follow our three basic rules:

- Always ask an adult's permission before using the internet.

- Never give out personal information, such as your name, address, the name of your school or telephone number.

- If a website asks you to type in your name or email address, check with an adult first.

For more information about using the internet, go to the Help and advice area at the Usborne Quicklinks website.

INDEX

In this index, page numbers in *italic* show where to find pictures. Words that have a lot of page numbers usually have a number in **bold** to show where to find the main explanation.

a

ablation zone **130**, 140
abyssal plain **134**, 140
abyssal zone **135**, 140
accumulation zone **130**, 140
acid rain 140
acids 116, 117, 124
active volcanoes 29, *36*, 140
adaptation 59, 60, 65, 67, 70, 73, 97, 98, **99**, 132, 140
aftershocks 41
agriculture ~ see farming
air
 ~ and breathing 99
 ~ currents in **50**, 51, 81, 82, 84
 ~ gases in 48, 49, 52, 53
 ~ in mountain areas 57, 72, 73, 130
 ~ and plants 96
 ~ and thunder 82-83
al-Idrisi 151
allergies 54
Alps 19
Amazon River 123, 126
ammonia 52
ammonites 21
Andes 19, *72*
animals 9, 20, 21, 24, 43, 52, 53, 55, 56, 64, 69, 73, 75, 80, 81, 85, 86, 87, 89, 96-103, **98**, 106-109, 112, 114, 116, 117, 122, 132
 ~ antelopes 101
 ~ aphids *109*
 ~ Arctic foxes *71*
 ~ badgers *98*
 ~ ballan wrasse fish *134*
 ~ bears, polar 70, 71
 ~ bees *79*
 ~ beetles *52*
 ~ bugs *99*
 ~ camels *65*
 ~ cats *103*
 ~ cheetahs *61*, *100*
 ~ colugos *59*
 ~ coral polyps 135, 141
 ~ cougars *72*
 ~ crabs 33, *133*
 ~ crocodiles *123*
 ~ deer *98*
 ~ dodos *103*
 ~ dogs *43*, *103*
 ~ dormice *69*
 ~ eagles *98*
 ~ earthworms *112*
 ~ earwigs *112*
 ~ egrets *122*
 ~ elephants *101*
 ~ fish *98*, *99*, *102*, 120-121, *134*, *135*, *136*, 137
 ~ flying lemurs *59*
 ~ frogs *91*, *95*
 ~ gazelles *61*, *100*
 ~ gerenuks *101*
 ~ giant pandas *98*
 ~ goats 72, *73*
 ~ golden lion tamarins *59*
 ~ guanacos *99*
 ~ hares *72*
 ~ hens *109*
 ~ herring *136*
 ~ hippopotamuses *122*
 ~ honeyeaters *98*
 ~ insects *52*, *59*, *61*, *98*, *109*
 ~ lemmings *100*
 ~ lions *61*
 ~ loggerhead turtles *135*
 ~ moose *57*
 ~ mosquitoes *63*
 ~ mountain goats *72*
 ~ musk oxen *70*
 ~ ostriches *61*, *107*
 ~ owls *100*
 ~ pandas *98*
 ~ penguins *70*
 ~ pigs *108*, *109*
 ~ polar bears 70, 71
 ~ salmon 120-121
 ~ sea bass *136*
 ~ seals *70*
 ~ sheep *72*
 ~ snakes *43*
 ~ snow leopards *103*
 ~ swordfish *135*
 ~ tsetse flies *61*
 ~ tubeworms *33*
 ~ warthogs *101*
 ~ wildebeest *61*
 ~ yaks *106*
 ~ zebras *98*
Antarctic (Antarctica) 49, **70**, 88, 131, 146
Antarctic Circle *15*, 68, *70*, **146**
Antarctic Ocean *70*
anti-cyclone 140
apatite 23
aquifer **128**, 140
arable farming **106**, 140
arches *132*
arcs, island *35*
Arctic 12, **70**, 71, 100, 146
Arctic Circle 10, *15*, 68, *70*, **146**
Arctic Ocean *70*
Aristotle 151
ash, volcanic **28**, 29, *31*, 34, *35*, *37*, 75
asteroids 74, 140

asthma 102
Atlantic Ocean 18, *51*, 123, *134*
atmosphere 13, **48-49**, 53, 54, 59, 74, 78, 79, 90, 140, 153
atmospheric pressure **50**, 92, *93*, 140, 151
atomic oxygen 49
atoms 25, **140**, 151
auroras 48, **90**, 140
 ~ australis 90, 140
 ~ borealis 90, 140
autumn *12*, 46-47, 68
AUV (Autonomous Underwater Vehicle) 140
axis *8*, 14, 140, 153

b

bacteria 33, *52*, 63, 112, 113, **140**
ball lightning *83*
basalt *17*
basalt lava *35*
Basque people *73*
beaches 35, *67*, 110-111, **132-133**
bedrock *113*, 140
billabongs *125*
biological pest control *109*
biological weathering 117
biomes 56, **101**, 140
birds 70, 75, 98, 103, 137
 ~ dodos *103*
 ~ eagles *98*
 ~ egrets *122*
 ~ hens *109*
 ~ honeyeaters *98*
 ~ ostriches *61*, *107*
 ~ owls *100*
 ~ penguins *70*
birth rate 104
black smokers *33*, 140
blast furnace *22*
blizzards 88
blocks, volcanic *28*
block mountains *19*
blue moon *149*
boats 86, *136*, *137*
 ~ fishing *136*
bombs, volcanic *28*, *29*
boundaries
 ~ constructive 18
 ~ destructive 18
 ~ fault *19*, 42
 ~ plate 18, 19, 30, 40
breathing 9, 48, 69, 80, **99**
breeding, selective 108, 145
buildings *2-3*, 23, 38, 39, *43*, 83, 84, *86*, *104*, *126*, 133, *152*

c

calcite *23*
calcium 22
calendars 148
camouflage 71, **98**, 140

canals *53*, **126**
Cancer, Tropic of 10, 12, 13, **146**
canopy *58*, 140
Capricorn, Tropic of 10, 12, 13, **146**
carbon 52, *53*
carbon cycle *53*, 54
carbon dioxide (CO_2) 53, **54**, 96
carnelian *21*
carnivores **98**, 100, 140
cars 54, 85, 88, 89, 102
cartography 10, 150
caves 117, 128, *129*, *132*, **138-139**
cement 23
CFCs (chlorofluorocarbons) 49, 140
chalk 20
charcoal *53*
chemical reactions 22, 25
chemicals 21, 22, 96, 101, 102, 109, 114, 116, 117, 137, 150
chemical weathering 116, 117, 129
chips, silicon 23
chlorofluorocarbons (CFCs) 49, 140
chlorophyll 96, 140
cholera 63
cirrus clouds *81*
cities *2-3*, 10, 38, 103, *126*, *152*
clay soil 24, **113**, *119*
cliffs *132*, *133*
climate 46-75, **56-57**, 78, 106, 131, 140, 150
climate change 11, 55, **74-75**, 131
climatology 150
clouds 48, 49, 54, 56, 57, 64, 66, 68, *72-73*, 79, **80-81**, 82, 84, 85, 87, 89, 90, 92
 ~ cirrus *81*
 ~ cumulonimbus *81*, *82*
 ~ cumulus *79*, *81*
 ~ lenticular *90*
 ~ stratus *81*
coal 24, 53, 54
coasts (see also beaches and seashore) 44, 45, 51, 60, 66, 67, 93, 131, **132-133**, 136
cold fronts 79
communities 100, 140
compass *17*, 140
computers 23, *79*, 92, *93*, 137, 155
concrete 23
condensation 80
cone volcanoes *28*
conservation **103**, 140
conservative margins 40
constructive boundaries 18
constructive waves 133

consumers 101
container ships *137*
continental climates 57, 69
continental crust *17*, 18, 140
continental ice sheets 131
continental shelf *134*, 140
continental slope *134*, 141
continents **18**, 60, 69, 75, 140, 151
conversion tables 154
coral reefs *135*, 141
core (Earth's) *16*, 17, 141
Coriolis effect 50, **84**, 85, 141
corundum 22, *23*
cover crops 115
craters, volcanic *28*, *34*
crescent moon *15*, *149*
crevasses *130*, 141
crop farming **106**, *107*, 108, *109*, 114
crop rotation 114, 141
crops 53, *59*, *63*, 67, 68, 78, 86, 87, **106**, *107*, 108, 109, *114*, 115
crust (Earth's) *16*, 17, 18, *19*, 20, 28, 30, 32, 34, 72, 75, 134, 141, 151
 ~ continental *17*, 18, 140
 ~ oceanic *17*, 18, *134*, 144
crystals 20
cumulonimbus clouds *81*, 82
cumulus clouds *79*, *81*
currents 30, 43, **50-51**, 66, 75, 81, 82, 85, 141
cycles, natural *52-53*, 148-149
cyclones 84, **93**, 141
cylindrical projection *147*

d

dams 86, *127*
Darwin, Charles 99, 151
Date Line, International 146, *147*
Davis, William Morris 151
death rate 104
debris *125*, 132, *133*, 141
deciduous trees 68, 69
decomposers *101*
deforestation 59, 115, 141
degrees 10, 141, **146**
deltas 122, **124**, 141
Democritus 151
deposition **124**, *125*, 141
depressions 68
desertification 65, 141
deserts 56, *57*, **64-65**, 72, 97, 100, 101
destructive boundaries 18
destructive waves *132*, 133
diamonds *23*
diseases 63, 87, 107, 109
Domesday Book *133*
dormant volcanoes 29, 141

156

drainage basins 123
droughts 51, 78, **87**, 92
drumlins *131*, 141
dry season 60, *62*, 86
Dust Bowl 87
dying out (see also extinction) 59, 99, 101, 103
dykes
 ~ sea 141
 ~ volcanic 28

e
earthquakes 11, *17*, 38-45, *38-39*, 91, 150, 151, 153
Earth sciences 150
ecology 150
ecosystems **100-101**, 102, 103, 109, 141
electrical currents 43
electricity 22, 24, 25, 37, 82, 88, 103, 127
electronic circuits 22
elements 21, 22, **141**
El Niño 51, 141
emergents *58*, 141
endangered species 59, 99, **103**
energy **24-25**, 55, 90, 101, 102, 103, 133
 ~ released by earthquakes 38, 40, 41
 ~ in lightning 82, 83
 ~ nuclear 24, *25*
 ~ from the Sun 13, 57, 89, 96
 ~ from waterpower 127
 ~ from wind 103
environment 71, 141
epicentre *41*
Equator 10, *12*, 13, *15*, 51, 60, 64, 66, 68, 75, 84, 92, 141, **146**, 147, 153
Eratosthenes 151
erosion 65, **118-119**, 151
 ~ of coasts 132, 133
 ~ by rivers 20, *124-125*
 ~ of rock 118, *119*, *124*, *125*, *130*, *132*, *133*
 ~ by the sea *132*, *133*
 ~ of soil 63, 65, 86, 87, 97, *115*, 118, *119*, *124*, 130
 ~ by wind 65, 87, 118
erratics 130, *131*, 141
eruptions, volcanic 11, *17*, *26-27*, **28**, 29, 30, 31, 32, 34, 35, 36, 44, 74, 75, 103, 141, 151, 153
estuaries 122, 141
evaporation 58, 79, **80**
evolution **99**, 141
exfoliation 117, 141
exosphere 48
extinction (see also dying out) 21, 99, **103**, 141
extinct volcanoes 29, 34, 141

f
factories 54, 102, 137
fallow land **114**, 141
famine 63, 78, 141
farming 37, 53, 54, 59, 61, *63*, 67, 68, 87, 102, 103, **106-109**, *114*, *115*, 126, 137
fault boundaries 19, 42
fault creep **42**, 141
faults *19*, 40, *42*, 141
fertility 37, 64, 68, 86, **112**, 113, 114, 141
fertilizer 53, 108, 109, ***114***, 142
fish 98, 99, 102, 135, 136, 137
 ~ ballan wrasse fish *134*
 ~ herring *136*
 ~ plaice *136*
 ~ salmon *120-21*
 ~ sea bass *136*
 ~ swordfish *135*
fishing 136
fissures 38
fjords *131*
floods 38, 44, 51, 55, 62, 63, 64, 78, ***86-87***, 127, 153
flowers 73, 96, 97, 98
fluorite *23*
fold mountains *19*, *72*, 73, 142
food
 ~ for animals 52, 53, 55, 61, 69, 97, **98**, 100, 101, 107, 109
 ~ for people 59, 63, 97, 102, 106-108, 114, 136
 ~ for plants 52, 53, ***96***, 97, 100, 101, 112
food chains 97, **100**, *101*, *102*, 135, 142
food webs **100**, 101, 102, 142
foreshocks 41
forests *46-47*, 54, 57, *58-59*, 68, *72*, 100, 106
fossil fuels **24**, 25, 53, 102, 127, 142
fossil record 75
fossils *21*, 24, 53, 75, 142, 150, 151
freeze-thaw action *117*, 142
freezing 64, 69, 70, 81, **88**, 117
Frigid Zone 68
frost 69, *76-77*
fuel 24, 53, 65, 103
full moon *15*, *149*
fungi 52, *101*, 112, 142

g
galaxies *9*, 74, 142, 153
gases 43, 102, 112, 116, 135
 ~ in the atmosphere 9, **48-49**, 59, 90
 ~ carbon dioxide (CO_2) 53, 54, 96
 ~ greenhouse 54, 55, 142
 ~ natural (fuel) 24, 38
 ~ nitrogen (N) 52, 53
 ~ oxygen (O) 49, 52, 53, 73, 96, 97, **99**
 ~ ozone 49
 ~ in stars 8
 ~ in volcanoes 28, 29, 31
gemstones *21*, *22*
geochemistry 150
geodimeter 36
geography 150
 ~ historical 150
 ~ regional 150
 ~ urban 150
geologists *17*, 18, 150, 151
geology 142, **150**, 151
geomorphology **150**, 151
geosciences 150
geostationary satellites **11**, 92, 142
geysers *32*, *33*, 142
gibbous moon *149*
gills 99
glacial valleys 75, 130, *131*, 142
glaciers 55, 74, 75, 122, ***130-131***, 142
glass 22, 23
global warming **54-55**, 59, 142
global winds 50
GMT (Greenwich Mean Time) 147
gold 22
gorges *20-21*, 124, *125*, 142
Gould, Stephen Jay 151
Grand Canyon *20-21*
granite *17*
grasslands ***60-61***, 68, 69, 101
gravity **48**, *118*, 133, 142, 149, 150
Great Rift Valley *19*
greenhouse effect *54*, 142
greenhouse gases **54**, 55, 142
Greenwich Mean Time (GMT) 147
groundwater 32, 33, 122, ***128-129***, 142
Gulf Stream *51*
gypsum *23*

h
habitats 55, 59, 74, 99, **100**, 101, 103, 142
hail 78, 79, 80, *81*, 88
hanging valleys *131*, 142
Hartshorne, Richard 151
Hawaiian-type eruptions *31*
headlands *132*
heat
 ~ in deserts 64, 65
 ~ from fossil fuels *25*
 ~ from inside the Earth 21, *37*
 ~ in mountain areas *72*
 ~ greenhouse 54, 55, 142
 ~ natural (fuel) 24, 38
 ~ nitrogen (N) 52, 53
 ~ oxygen (O) 49, 52, 53, 73, 96, 97, **99**
 ~ ozone 49
 ~ in stars 8
 ~ in volcanoes 28, 29, 31
heat expansion 50, 79, 117, 142
heatstroke 89
heatwave 89
Henry the Navigator 151
HEP (hydroelectric power) ***127***, 142
herbivores 61, **98**, 100, 142
hibernation 69
high tide 133, *149*
Himalayas *19*, 106, *118*
homelessness 105
Homolosine projection *147*
horizons *113*, 142
hot spots *30*, *32*, *34*, 142
hot springs (see also thermal springs) *1*, *32*, 33, 142
humans (see also people) 25, 53, 61, 98, 102, 103, 118, 126
Humboldt, Alexander von 151
humidity 58, 62, **89**, 142
humus **112**, 113, 114, 142
hurricanes **84**, 85, 91, *92-93*, 153
Hutton, James 151
hydroelectric power (HEP) ***127***, 142
hydrothermal vents *33*, 142

i
ice 70, 74, *76-77*, 80, 81, 82, 86, 88, 117, 122, 130, 131
Ice ages **74**, 75, 142, 143
icebergs *4*, *131*, 142
icecaps, polar 55
ice sheets, continental 131, 142
ice storms 78, **88**
igneous rock **20**, 21, 142
imperial measurements 154
impermeable rock **128**, 143
infrared light 11, 143
insects 59, 98
 ~ aphids *109*
 ~ bees 79
 ~ beetles *52*
 ~ bugs 99
 ~ earwigs *112*
 ~ mosquitoes *63*
 ~ tsetse flies *61*
intensive farming 108, **109**, 143
interglacials 74, 143
International Date Line 146, *147*
Inuit 88
iron 16, 17, **22**
irrigation 67, 126
irrigation canals 126
island arcs 35
 ~ in rainforests 58
 ~ from the Sun 8, 9, *12*, 13, 54, 56, 57, 74, 80, 89, 96
 ~ and weathering 117
heat expansion 50, 79, 117, 142
heatstroke 89
heatwave 89
Henry the Navigator 151
HEP (hydroelectric power) ***127***, 142
islands 18, 124, 152
 ~ volcanic *34-35*
isobars *93*, 143

j
Jupiter *8*, 149

k
K2 *118*
Kant, Immanuel 151

l
Labrador current *51*
lakes 80, 86, 122, 128, 129, 152
 ~ oxbow *125*, 144
Land of the Midnight Sun *15*
landslides 20, 78, **119**, 143
land use 11, *106*
lasers *42*
latitude 10, 56, 57, 143, **146**, 151
lava *26-27*, **28**, 29, 30, 31, 34, 35, *75*, 143
leap years 13, 143, **148**
leaves 58, 59, 65, 67, 68, *69*, 80, **96**
lenticular clouds *90*
life (see also plants, animals and living things) 9, 13, 52, 97, 112, 135
light 8, 9, 12, 13, 14, 15, 58, 90, 96, 101
 ~ infrared 11, 143
 ~ ultraviolet 49, 143
lightning *82-83*
limestone 21, 22, 117, 129
lithium 22
litter 137
livestock farming **106**, 107, 108, 109
living things (see also plants, animals and life) 9, 52, 74, 75, 96, 97, 112, 150
loam soil 113
longitude 10, 143, **146**, 147, 151
low tide *149*
lungs 99
L-waves 41
Lyell, Sir Charles 151

m
Mackinder, Halford J. 151
magma **16**, 18, 20, 21, *28*, 30, 32, 34, 35, 143
magma chamber *28*
magnesium 16
magnetic fields 17, 74, 150
magnetic poles 17, 143
magnets 17, 143
malaria 63, 143
mantle **16**, 18, 28, 30, 143
manure 114, 143
maps **10**, 11, *18*, *56*, *58*, *60*, *64*, *66*, *68*, *70*, *74*, *92*, *93*, *105*, ***146-147***, 150, 151
marble *21*, *23*

maritime climates 57
Mars 8
meanders 122, 123, **125**, 143
measurement systems 154
medicines 97, 99, 104
Mediterranean climates **66-67**, 143
Mediterranean Sea 66, 67, 123, 126
meltwater 130
Mercalli scale 39
Mercator projection 147
Mercury 8
meridians 146
mesopause 48
mesosphere 48, 49
metals 22, 25
~ precious 22
metamorphic rock 20, 21, 143
meteorology 92, 93, 143, 150, 151
meteors 48
metric measurements 154
mica schist 21
mid-latitudes 68
Midnight Sun, Land of 15
migration 61, 69, 143
Milky Way 9, 153
mineralogy 150
minerals 21, 22, 23, 24, 32, 33, 37, 112, 113, 114, 128, 129, 135, 143, 150, 151
mineral water 128
mining 24
minutes 146
mirage 143
mixed farming 106
Mohs scale 23
molecule 143
moment magnitude scale 39, 153
monsoons **62-63**, 81, 143
monsoon season 62
month 149
Moon, the 7, **9**, 15, 133, 148, 149, 151
moons 9, 143, 149
moraine **130**, 131, 143
mountain ranges 10, 18, 19, 30, 33, 72
mountains 19, 57, 65, **72-73**, 86, 100, 106, 117, 118, 119, 122, 130, 134, 152
~ block 19
~ fold 19, 72, 73, 142
mud 124, 150

n
nagana 61
natural selection **99**, 143, 151
navigable rivers 126, 143
nectar 98
Neptune 8
nets, fishing 136
new moon 15, 149

Niagara Falls 124-125
niche 101, 143
nickel 16
Nile River 86, 123
nitrates 52, 53, **114**, 143
nitrogen (N) 52, 53
nitrogen cycle 52, 53
North Atlantic Drift 51
Northern Lights (see also aurora borealis) 90
North Pole 17, 70, 143, 146
nuclear energy 24, 25
nuclear power 25, 137, 143

o
oases 64, 144
obsidian 20
ocean currents 51, 75
ocean floor (see also seabed) 10, 18, 134
oceanic crust 17, 18, 134, 144
oceanic ridges 18, 134, 144
oceanic trenches 18, 134, 144
oceanography 134, 144, 150, 151
oceans (see also seas) 18, 93, 122, 132, **134-135**, 136, 137, 150, 152
~ Antarctic 70
~ Arctic 70
~ Atlantic 18, 51, 123, 134
~ and climate 55, 56, 57, 62, 69
~ currents in 50, 51
~ Pacific 45, 50, 51, 146
~ and tides 133, **149**
oil 24, 25, 53, 54, 137
oil platforms 24-25
omnivores 98, 144
opal 21
opencast mining 24
orbiting 8, 9, 11, 12, 13, 14, 15, 74, 92, 144, 148, 149, 153
ores 22, 25, 144
organic farming 109, 144
organic matter 112
organisms 96, 112, 117, 144, 150
organizations 155
orthoclase 23
outcrops 117, 144
oxbow lakes 125, 144
oxygen (O) 52, 53, 73, 96, 97, **99**
~ atomic 49
ozone 49, 144
ozone hole 49
ozone layer 49, 144

p
Pacific Ocean 45, 50, 51, 146
paddy fields 63, 106
Pangaea 18, 144, 151

parallels 146
parasites 61
pastoral farming 106, 144
pebbles **110-111**, 124, 132, 133
pedology 150
people (see also humans) 9, 56, 63, 64, 65, 73, 97, 136
~ Basque 73
~ breathing 80, 99
~ and earthquakes 38, 39, 42, 43
~ and pollution 55, 102, 103
~ population 104, 105
~ in rainforests 59
~ Tuareg 65
~ and volcanoes 36, 37
~ and weather 53, 78, 85, 86, 87, 88, 89
permafrost 70, 144
pest control, biological 109
pesticides 108
Peters projection 147
phases of the Moon 15, 149
photosynthesis **96**, 100, 144
physical weathering 116, 117
pipes, volcanic 28
plains 60
planets 8, 9, 96, 144, 149, 153
plants 9, 20, 21, 24, 52, 53, 54, 55, 56, 59, 64, 65, 68, 69, 70, 73, 74, 75, 79, 80, 81, 86, 96-103, **96**, 106, 108, 112, 113, 114, 115, 116, 117, 122, 132, 133, 135, 137, 151
~ acacia trees 60-61
~ algae 53
~ aloes 97
~ alpine forget-me-nots 73
~ annual plants 69
~ cactuses 97
~ citrus fruits 67
~ clover 114
~ cork oak trees 67
~ fungi 52, 101, 112, 142
~ giant sequoia trees 97
~ grasses 60, 69, 87, 101, 108
~ legumes 114
~ lichens 117, 143
~ maple trees 56
~ oilseed rape 114
~ olive trees 67
~ orange trees 67
~ parsnips 113
~ peas 52
~ perennial plants 69
~ phytoplankton 135
~ sunflowers 96, 97
~ trees 43, 46-47, 56, 58-59, 60-61, 62-63, 67, 83, 84, 88, 97, 101, 114, 115, 119
plastic 25, 102, 137

plate boundaries 18, 19, 30, 40
plates **18**, 19, 30, 35, **40**, 43, 72, 75, 118, 144
plate tectonics 144, 151
Plinian-type eruptions 31
Pliny 91
polar icecaps 55
polar regions 70-71
poles 13, 50, 51, 68, **70**, 71, 90, 131, 144, **146**
~ magnetic 17, 143
~ North 17, 70, 143, 146
~ South 17, 70, 75, 145, 146
pollen 54
pollution 48, 53, 54, 55, **102-103**, 109, 114, 127, 136, 137, 144
Pompeii 29
population **104-105**, 144
population control 104
porous rock 64, 128, 144
ports 126, 144
poverty 105
power stations 25, 37, 54, 137
prairies 69
precious metals 22
precious stones 21, 22
precipitation 81, 144
predators 61, 70, 71, **98**, 99, 107, 133
prey 71, 98, 99
primary consumers 101
Prime Meridian Line 10, 144, **146**
producers 101
projections 10, 144, **147**
Ptolemy 151
P-waves 41
Pyrenees 73

q
quarries 23
quarters, Moon's 15, 149
quartz 23

r
radar 11, 92, 144
radiation 25, 144
~ infrared 11, 143
~ ultraviolet 49, 145
radioactivity 25, 137, 144
radio waves 11
rain 32, 78, 79, **80**, 81, 88, 92, 93, 112, 116, 122, 124, 128
~ and climate 57, 58, 60, 64, 67, 68, 72
~ and droughts 87
~ and erosion 115, 118, 119
~ and flooding 86
~ frog showers 91
~ monsoon 62, 63
rain clouds 80, 81, 87, 92
rain dance 78
rainfall 57, 66, 69, 92

rainforests **58-59**, 101
rain shadow 72
rainstorms 55
rainy season 60, 62, 86
reactions
~ chemical 22, 25
~ nuclear 25
Red Sea 126, 135
remote-operated vehicle (ROV) 134, 144
remote sensing 11, 144
renewable energy 127
reproduction 97
resources **22-23**, 103, 150
rice 63, 106
ridges
~ oceanic 18, 134, 144
~ spreading 30
rift valleys 19, 144
Ring of Fire 144
riots 89
Ritter, Carl 151
River Amazon 123, 126
River Nile 86, 123
rivers 79, 80, 91, 100, 118, **120-127**, 128, 129, 130, 152
~ and droughts 86
~ erosion by 20, 124-125
~ and floods 86
~ pollution of 53, 114
~ ports on 126
Robinson projection 147
rockfalls 118
rocks 16, 17, 19, **20-21**, 22, 23, 24, 40, 41, 43, 65, 75, 122, 123, 126, 134, 146, 149, 150, 151
~ erosion of 118, 119, 124, 125, 130, 132, 133
~ igneous 20, 21, 142
~ impermeable 128, 143
~ metamorphic 20, 21, 143
~ meteors 48
~ porous 64, 128, 144
~ sedimentary 20, 21, 145, 150
~ in soil 112, 113
~ volcanic 28, 32, 37
~ weathering of 116, 117
roots 65, 73, **96**, 97, 112, 113, 117

s
salt 22
sand 20, 22, **23**, 24, 35, 65, 124, 133
sand-blasting 65
sandstone 20, 128
sandstorms 65
sandy soil 113
satellite images **11**, 50, 51, 56, 84, 92-93, 124
satellites 9, **11**, 56, 79, 92, 93, 136, 144
Saturn 8, 9
scale (on maps) 10
schist 127

scientists 99, *134*, **150-151**
scree 118
seabed 24, 30, 33, 34, 35, 44, 124, **134**, 150
sea birds 70, *137*
sea level 55, 74
seas (*see also* oceans) 79, 84, 85, 97, 100, 118, 124, 131, 132, **134-137**, 149, 150
~ and climate 66, 67, 70, 71
~ erosion by 132, 133
~ and flooding 86
~ and global warming 55
~ Mediterranean 66, 67, 123, 126
~ and oil 24
~ Red 126, *135*
~ temperature of 51, 55, *92*
~ and tsunamis 44, 45
~ and underwater volcanoes 33, 34, 35, 44
seashore 132-133
seasons **12**, 13, 60, 62, 63, 68, 69
secondary consumers 101
seconds 146
sediment 20, 21, 124, 125
sedimentary rock **20**, 21, 145, 150
sedimentology 150
seeds 69, 96, *97*, 101, 108
seismic gaps 42
seismic waves 17, 39, **41**
seismogram 17, 39
seismology 39, 145, 150
seismometer 36, *39*
selective breeding 108, 145
sewage 137, 145
shale 119
shanty towns 104-105, 145
shield volcanoes 28
ships 91, 126, *137*
siestas 89
silicon 16, 22, 23
silicon chips 23
silt soil 113
silver 22
skyfalls 91
skyscrapers *2-3*, 43
slash-and-burn *59*, 145
sleeping sickness 61
smog *102-103*, 145
snow 56, 57, 70, 71, 72, 78, 79, **80**, 81, 86, 88, 93, 122, *128*, 130, 131
soil 11, 37, 68, 69, 79, 87, 96, 101, **112-115**, 116, 128, 150
~ clay 24, **113**, 119
~ erosion of 63, 65, 86, 87, 97, *115*, 118, *119*, 124, 130
~ and farming 53, 106, 107
~ loam 113
~ and nitrates 52, 53
~ sandy 113
~ silt 113
soil science 150
solar flares 90
solar system 8, 74, 145, 153
solar year 13, 145, **148**
sonar **134**, 136, 145
South pole *17*, 70, 75, 145, *146*
space *6-7*, **8-9**, 10, 54, 74, 90, 92, 150, 153
spiracles 99
spiral eddies *50*
spraying (crops) 108, *109*
spreading ridges 30
spring (season) **12**, 68
springs 128
~ hot or thermal *1*, *32-33*, 145
spring water 128
stacks 132
stalactites *129*, **138-139**, 145
stalagmites *129*, **138-139**, 145
stars *8*, *9*, 145, 151
stems 65, *96*
steppes 69
stomata *96*, 145
storms 51, 78, 79, **82-85**, 86, 88, 91, 92, 93, 153
~ on the Sun 90
Strabo 151
strange weather 90-91
strata *20-21*, 145, 151
stratopause 48
stratosphere *48*, 49
stratus clouds *81*
stress (in the Earth's crust) 40, 42, 43
subduction zones 30, 35, 145
submersibles 134, 145
subsoil *113*, 145
Suez Canal 126
summer **12**, 66, 67, 68, 69, 71
Sun, the **8**, 48, 49, 50, 51, 74, *90*, 117, 148, 153
~ and climate 56, 57, 58, 60, 62, 64, 68, 74
~ energy from 13, 57, 89, 96
~ and global warming 54
~ at Midnight *15*
~ and the Moon 15, 149
~ and plants **96**, 100, *101*, 135
~ and the seasons *12-13*, 60, 62
~ and the solar system *8*
~ and tourism 67
~ and weather 79, 89, 93
sunless zone *135*
sunlit zone *135*
sustainable living 103
S-waves 41

t
talc 22, *23*
tea 63
technology 10, 78, 104, 109, 136
teeth *98*
temperate climates 56, 57, 66, 67, **68-69**, 145
Temperate Zone 68
temperature 13, 57, 154
~ of the atmosphere 48, 49, 50
~ and climate 64, 68, 72, 73
~ of the sea 51, 55, *92*
~ and weather 78, **79**, 88, 89, 92
~ and weathering 117
terraces *106-107*, 115, 145
tertiary consumers 101
thermal spring *1*, *32-33*, 145 (*see also* hot spring)
thermosphere *48*, 49
thunder 82, 83
thunderstorms 62, **82-83**, 85
tidal wave 145
tides 132, 133, 145, 148, **149**
tiltmeter 36, *42*
time 154
time zones *147*
topaz *23*
topsoil *113*, 145
Tornado Alley 85
tornadoes 84, *85*, 91, 153
Torrid Zone 68
tourism 67
trade winds **50**, 60
transpiration 145
transport 126, 136, *137*
treeline 72, 145
trees 43, *46-47*, 56, *58-59*, *60-61*, *62-63*, 67, 83, 84, 88, *97*, 101, 114, *115*, 119
~ acacia *60-61*
~ and coal 24
~ cork oak 67
~ deciduous 68, *69*
~ giant sequoia *97*
~ maple *56*
~ olive 67
~ orange *67*
tremors 36, 41, 150
trenches, oceanic *18*, 134, 144
tribes 59
tributaries 122, 145
trophic levels 101
tropical deserts *64-65*
tropical grasslands 56, *60-61*
tropical rainforests *58-59*
Tropic of Cancer 10, 12, 13, **146**
Tropic of Capricorn 10, 12, 13, **146**
tropics 50, 56, 58, 62, 66, 68, 84, 135, 145, **146**
tropopause 48

troposphere *48*, 50
tsunami **44-45**, 91, 145
Tuareg people *65*
tuff 20
tundra 70, 145
turbines 37, 103, 127, 145
turquoise *21*
twilight zone *135*
typhoid 63
typhoons ~ *see* hurricanes

u
ultraviolet (UV) light 49, 145
understorey *58*, 145
universe, the 8, 9, 153
uranium *25*
Uranus *8*

v
vacations 66, 67, 78
valleys 122, 134
~ glacial 75, *131*, 142
~ hanging *131*, 142
~ rift *19*, 144
Varenius, Bernhardus 151
vegetation 11, 56, 59, 60, 65, 67, 68, 72
vents
~ hydrothermal *33*, 142
~ volcanic *28*
Venus *8*
volcanic ash *28*, 29, *31*, 34, *35*, 37, 75
volcanic blocks *28*
volcanic bombs *28*, 29
volcanic craters *28*, 34
volcanic eruptions 11, 17, *26-27*, **28**, 29, 30, 31, 32, 34, 35, 36, 44, 74, 75, 103, 141, 151, 153
volcanic islands *34-35*
volcanic vents *28*
volcanoes (*see also* volcanic eruptions) **26-37**, 118, 134, 150, 151
~ active *29*, 36, 140
~ cone *28*
~ dormant 29, 141
~ extinct 29, 34, 141
~ shield *28*
volcanology 145, 150

w
waning moon *15*, 149
water 9, 35, 43, 44, 45, 52, 58, 60, 63, 64, 65, 67, 79, **80**, 81, 86, 87, 92, 118, 132, 149
~ and animals 98, 99
~ bottled *128*
~ in clouds 54, *80*, *81*, *82*, 83
~ energy from 127
~ erosion by 23, 116, *117*, 118, 119, *124*, 125, *132*, *133*
~ in extracting fuels 24
~ in farming 106, 107
~ in geysers 32, 33
~ in the ground *32*, 33, *37*, 122, **128-129**, 142
~ and plants 96, 97
~ in rivers 122-127
~ in seas and oceans 50, 51, 55, *132-135*
~ in soil 112, 113
water cycle **80**, 151
waterfalls 122, 124, **125**, 129, 152
waterpower 127
waterspouts *85*, 151
water table *128*, 145
waterwheel *127*
waves *44-45*, 91, **132**, 133
waxing moon *15*, 149
weather 11, 48, 51, 56, 72, **76-92**, 116, 150, 151
weather forecasting 79, **92-93**, 150
weathering **116-117**, 118, 129
weather stations 92, 93
weather systems 79
Web sites 155
Wegener, Alfred 151
wheat *107*, 108
wind (*see also* hurricanes *and* tornadoes) 50, 51, 55, 60, 66, 70, 72, 73, 78, 79, **84-85**, 88, 92, 97, 109
~ energy from 103
~ erosion by 65, 87, 118
~ monsoon 62
windstorms (*see also* hurricanes *and* tornadoes) 84-85
wind turbines 103
wine 67
winter **12**, 66, 68, 69, 88

y
years 148
~ leap 13, 143, 148
~ solar 13, 145, 148
yellow fever 63
yield 108, 109, 145

z
zoos 103

ACKNOWLEDGEMENTS

Every effort has been made to trace the copyright holders of the material in this book. If any rights have been omitted, the publishers offer to rectify this in any subsequent edition, following notification. The publishers are grateful to the following organizations and individuals for their contributions and permission to reproduce material (t=top, m=middle, b=bottom, l=left, r=right):

Cover Desert image © Jamie Harron; Papilio/CORBIS; all other images Digital Vision; endpapers CORBIS/Wolfgang Kaehler; p1 CORBIS/Yann Arthus-Bertrand; p2 CORBIS/Joseph Sohm, ChromoSohm Inc; p4 CORBIS/Ralph A. Clevenger; p6 © Digital Vision; p8 (l) © Digital Vision; (tr) Gary Bines; (br) Jeremy Gower; p9 (tr) NASA; p10 (tl and br) © Map Creation Ltd; (bl) © Digital Vision; p11 (tr) © ESA–P. Carril; (br) © Digital Vision; p12 (tr) © Digital Vision; (ml) CORBIS/Dave G. Houser; (mr) © Digital Vision; (b) Jeremy Gower; p13 (mr and bl) © Digital Vision; (br) CORBIS/Bill Ross; p14 (bl) Jeremy Gower; (tr and br) © Digital Vision; p15 (tl) Chris Lyon; (tr) Gary Bines; (b) Simon Fraser/Science Photo Library; p16 (main) © Digital Vision; (insert) Gary Bines; p17 (tl) Jeremy Gower; (mr) Andy Burton; (bl) Chris Lyon; (br) Howard Allman; p18 (tr) Jeremy Gower; (mr) Guy Smith; (br) Jeremy Gower; p19 (tr) Guy Smith; (mr) CORBIS/Yann Arthus-Bertrand; (br) CORBIS/Galen Rowell; p20 (main) G.S.F Picture Library © Dr. B. Booth; (ml, m, tr and mr) Mike Freeman; p21 Mike Freeman; p22 (bl) CORBIS/Kevin Fleming; (tr) Jeremy Gower; p23 (l) Mike Freeman and Roberto de Gugliemo/Science Photo Library; (tr) Rosenfeld Images Ltd/Science Photo Library; (br) CORBIS/Dorothy Burrows, Eye Ubiquitous; p24 (main image and bl) © Digital Vision; p25 (tr) © Digital Vision; (br) Laura Fearn; p26 CORBIS/Douglas Peebles; p28 G.S.F. Picture Library © Dr. B. Booth; (bl and mr) Jeremy Gower; (br) Chris Shields; p29 (br) Chris Shields; p30 (bl, tr, br) Jeremy Gower; (tl) © Digital Vision; p31 (bl) © Digital Vision © Superstock; p32 (main) CORBIS/Michael T. Sedam; (tr) Jeremy Gower; p33 (tl) CORBIS/Ralph White; (br) D. Drain/Still Pictures; p34 (main) CORBIS/Amos Nachoum; (b) Jeremy Gower; p35 (tr) G.S.F. Picture Library © Solarfilm A; (b) CORBIS/Douglas Peebles; p36 (main) G.S.F. Picture Library © Univ. California; (bl) CORBIS/Philip James Corwin; p37 (br) Jeremy Gower; pp38–39 (main) © Chien-Min Chung/In Pictures/CORBIS; (tr) CORBIS/Grant Smith; p39 (tl) Photo courtesy of Kinemetrics Inc; (r) Peter Bull; p40 (main) CORBIS/Kevin Schafer; (ml, bl and br) Jeremy Gower; p41 Jeremy Gower; p42 (t) Jeremy Gower; (b) CORBIS/Roger Ressmeyer; p43 (bl) Jane Burton; (r) CORBIS/Richard Cummins; p44 (tr) © Dinodia Photos/Alamy; (b) Jeremy Gower; p45 (tr) Jeremy Gower; (b) FOTO-UNEP/Still Pictures; p46 CORBIS/Scott T. Smith; p48 (main) George Hall; (tl) © Digital Vision; (l) CORBIS/Jonathan Blair; (ml) NASA; (b) © Digital Vision; p49 (tr) GSFC/NASA; p50 (b) NASA/Science Photo Library; p51 (t) Los Alamos National Laboratory/Science Photo Library; (background and bl) Shuttle Views the Earth: Oceans from Space, compiled by Pat Jones and Gordon Wells, courtesy of LPI; p52 (tr) Dr. Jeremy Burgess/Science Photo Library; (mr) Peter Bull; (bl) CORBIS/Karl Switak, ABPL; p53 (tl) Nick Cobbing/Still Pictures; (mr) CORBIS/Chinch Gryniewicz, Ecoscene; (bl) Peter Bull; p54 (main) CORBIS/Vince Streano; (tr) CORBIS/Ron Boardman, Frank Lane Picture Agency (bl) © Digital Vision; p55 (t) CORBIS/Wolfgang Kaehler; p56 (tr) CORBIS/Dewitt Jones; (m) PLI/Science Photo Library; p57 (bl) CORBIS/Paul A. Souders; (br) © Digital Vision; p58 (main) CORBIS/Reinhard Eisele; (bl) Nicola Butler; p59 (tr) © Digital Vision; (ml, mr and bl) Ian Jackson; p60 (main) CORBIS/Buddy Mays; (tr) Nicola Butler; p61 (t) CORBIS/Buddy Mays; (mr) Ian Jackson; (br) CORBIS/Anthony Bannister, ABPL; p62 (main) CORBIS/Kit Kittle; (bl) Jeremy Gower; p63 (ml) Yann Layma/Getty Images; (tr) David Scharf/Science Photo Library; p64 (main) CORBIS/Christine Osborne; (tr) Nicola Butler; (mr) CORBIS/Jeremy Horner; p65 (mr) Ian Jackson; p66 (tr) Nicola Butler; (bl) CORBIS/Gail Mooney; p67 (tr and b) Carlos Guarita/Still Pictures; (ml) Kathy Collins/Getty Images; p68 (tl) Nicola Butler; (r) CORBIS/Stuart Westmoreland; p69 (tl) CORBIS/Ron Watts; (tr) CORBIS/Stuart Westmoreland; (br) CORBIS/George MacCarthy; p70 (tl, tr, bl and br) Ian Jackson; p71 (t) CORBIS/Dan Guravich; (b) CORBIS/Paul A. Souders; p72 (main) CORBIS/Galen Rowell; (tr) CORBIS/David Muench; p73 (tr) CORBIS/William A. Bake; (br) CORBIS/Catherine Karnow; p74 (main) © Digital Vision; (tr) Arc Science Simulations/Science Photo Library; p75 (tr) Kevin Schafer/Still Pictures; (bl) © Digital Vision; p76 CORBIS/Steve Kaufman; p78 (background) CORBIS/Craig Aurness; (l) CORBIS/Michael Yamashita; (tr) Ian Jackson; p79 (t) © Digital Vision; (ml) Ian Jackson; (b) CORBIS/Wolfgang Kaehler; p80 (tr) Scott Camazine/Science Photo Library; (bl) Peter Dennis; p81 (background, tl and tr) Shuttle Views the Earth: Clouds from Space, compiled by Pat Jones, courtesy of LPI; (ml) CORBIS/Wolfgang Kaehler; (bl) © Digital Vision; (br) Ian Jackson; pp82-83 (main) Glen Allison/Getty Images; (bl) Shuttle Views the Earth: Clouds from Space, compiled by Pat Jones, courtesy of LPI; p83 (tr) Werner Burger/Fortean Picture Library; p84 (tr) NOAA; pp84-85 (main) John Lund/Getty Images; p85 (br) Library of Congress; (b) Guy Smith; p86 (main) CORBIS/Michael S. Yamashita; (tr) Shuttle Views the Earth: Geology from Space, compiled by Peter Francis and Pat Jones, courtesy of LPI; p87 (tr and ml) © Digital Vision; p88 (tr) Michael Sewell/Still Pictures; (bl) Robert H. Pearson, Canada; p89 (tr) Seymour Snowman Sun Protection Campaign, NSW Cancer Council and NSW Health Department, Sydney, Australia, 1997/8; (bl) Will and Deni McIntyre/Getty Images; (br) CORBIS/Peter Turnley; p90 (main) Pekka Parviainen/Science Photo Library; (tr) Magrath/Folsom/Science Photo Library; (bl) © Digital Vision; p91 Llewellyn Publications/Fortean Picture Library; (mr) CORBIS/Alamay and E. Vicens; p92 (main and tr) © Digital Vision; (bl) European Space Agency; p93 (tr) Courtesy of International Weather Productions; p94 CORBIS/Michael and Patricia Fogden; p96 (tl, tr, bl) © Digital Vision; (br) CORBIS/Ron Boardman, Frank Lane Picture Agency; p97 (tl) © Digital Vision; (r) CORBIS/Galen Rowell; (bl) Howard Allman; p98 (main) CORBIS/Stuart Westmoreland; (ml) Ian Jackson; (bl and br) Chris Shields; p99 (tr, mr and b) Ian Jackson; (br) Jeremy Gower; p100 (tr) Ian Jackson; (ml) CORBIS/Tom Brakefield; (br) David Wright; p101 (tl and r) © Digital Vision; p102 (main and bl) © Digital Vision; p103 (tr) © Digital Vision (ml) Michael Viard/Still Pictures; (br) Ian Jackson; p104 (main) CORBIS/Hans Georg Roth; (tr) Ron Giling/Robert Harding; p105 (m) Craig Asquith; p106 (main) CORBIS/Keren Su; (tr) Fiona Patchett and Laura Fearn; (ml) Ian Jackson; p107 CORBIS/W. Wayne Lockwood, M.D.; (mr) Ian Jackson; p108 (tr and bl) Ian Jackson; (br) Rachel Lockwood; p109 (tr) CORBIS/Richard Hamilton Smith; (bl) Ian Jackson; (br) © Digital Vision; p110 CORBIS/Ric Ergenbright; p112 (tr) CORBIS/Robert Pickett; (bl) CORBIS/Ken Wilson, Papilio; p113 (tl) Andrew Beckett; (tr) CORBIS/Michael Boys; (b) CORBIS/Bob Rowan, Progressive Image; p114 (tr) CORBIS/Richard Hamilton Smith; (b) CORBIS/Eric Crichton; p115 (tl) CORBIS/Dean Conger; (tr) Ancient Art and Architecture; (b) Alan Watson/Still Pictures; p116 (main) CORBIS/John Farmer, Cordaiy Photo Library Ltd; p117 (tr) Jeremy Gower; (br) CORBIS/Robert Holmes; p118 (main) CORBIS/Layne Kennedy; (tr) Jeremy Gower; p119 (tl) CORBIS/Richard A. Cooke; (br) CORBIS/Wolfgang Kaehler; p120 CORBIS/Lawson Wood; p122 (tr and bl) © Digital Vision; (br) Ian Jackson; p123 (tl) Shuttle Views the Earth: Geology from Space, compiled by Peter Francis and Pat Jones, courtesy of LPI; (tr) Mint Images/Frans Lanting/Getty Images; (b) © Digital Vision; p124 (main) CORBIS/John and Dallas Heaton; (tr) CORBIS/Digital Image ©1996 CORBIS; original image courtesy of NASA; (bl) CORBIS/David Muench; p125 (tl and br) Jeremy Gower; p126 (tr) Mansell Collection/Visscher; (m) CORBIS/Charles and Josette Lenars; p127 (tl) CORBIS/Michael T. Sedam; (tr) CORBIS/Charles and Josette Lenars; (b) CORBIS/Philip James Corwin; p128 (t) Evian Natural Mineral Water; (tr) Photography courtesy of The Strathmore Mineral Water Co; (bl) Jeremy Gower; p129 (tr) CORBIS/Richard Hamilton Smith; (b) CORBIS/Macduff Everton; p130 (main) CORBIS/Neil Rabinowitz; (bl) Chris Lyon; p131 (t) Jeremy Gower; (mr) CORBIS/Ralph A. Clevenger; p132 (background) © Digital Vision; (ml) Laura Fearn; (bl) Chris Lyon; (mr) © Markus Keller/imageBROKER/Corbis; p133 (tr) CORBIS/Anthony Bannister, ABPL; (b) © Digital Vision; p134 (tl) CORBIS/Lawson Wood; (m) Dr. Ken McDonald/Science Photo Library; (b) CORBIS/Amos Nachoum; p135 (tl and b) © Digital Vision; (tr) Peter Dennis; p136 (main, tr and ml) CORBIS/Michael S. Yamashita; p137 (tl) CORBIS/Charles O'Rear; (br) © Digital Vision; p138 CORBIS/David Muench; p140, p142, p144 © Digital Vision; p146 (tr) Map Creation Ltd; (bl) Nicola Butler; p147 Nicola Butler; p149 Susannah Owen/Nicola Butler; p150 © Digital Vision; p152 and p154 © Digital Vision.

This edition edited by Phil Clarke and Kirsteen Robson

This edition first published in 2015 by Usborne Publishing Ltd, 83-85 Saffron Hill, London EC1N 8RT, England. www.usborne.com Copyright © 2015, 2008, 2003, 1999 Usborne Publishing Ltd. The name Usborne and the devices ♀ ♃ are Trade Marks of Usborne Publishing Ltd. All rights reserved. No part of this publication may be reproduced, stored in a retrieval system, or transmitted in any form or by any means, electronic, mechanical, photocopying, recording or otherwise, without the prior permission of the publisher. UE. Printed in the UAE.

Usborne Publishing is not responsible and does not accept liability for the availability or content of any website other than its own, or for any exposure to harmful, offensive, or inaccurate material which may appear on the Web. Usborne Publishing will have no liability for any damage or loss caused by viruses that may be downloaded as a result of browsing the sites it recommends. Usborne downloadable pictures are the copyright of Usborne Publishing Ltd. and may not be reproduced in print or in electronic form for any commercial or profit-related purpose.

FALCONRIDGE SCHOOL

FALCONRIDGE SCHOOL